IDEAS ON DEMAND

A Crash Course on Creativity

Bust creativity blocks

10x your ideas

become an ideas machine

MILIIND HARRDAS

Disclaimer

The author and publisher of the book have used their best efforts in preparing this material. The author and publisher make no representation or warranties with respect to the accuracy, applicability, or completeness of the contents. They disclaim any warranties (expressed or implied) or merchantability for any particular purpose.

Copyright ©2021 Miliind Harrdas

All Rights Reserved. No part of this book may be reproduced, used, or distributed in any form, electronic or print, without the prior written permission of the author, except for small quotations /excerpts with reference to the book/author. The information presented in this publication is compiled from sources believed to be accurate; however, both the publisher and author assume no responsibility for errors or omissions.

Table of Content

Preface 6

Section # 1 - Introduction 10

   Creativity – Your long lever for 10x impact 11

   How will this book help you to unleash your creativity? 15

   How is this book structured? 19

   Who is this book for? 27

<u>**Section # 2 -**</u> **Removing Creativity Blocks** 33

   Chapter 1 — *"Creativity Is Not My Cup Of Tea"* 34

   Chapter 2 — *"Don't Ask Stupid Questions"* 40

   Chapter 3 — *"First, I Want Complete Clarity"* 49

   Chapter 4 — *"What's the right answer?"* 58

   Chapter 5 — *"Be practical"* 68

<u>**Section # 3 -**</u> **Connecting the Dots** 76

   Chapter 6 — *Creativity is all about connecting the dots* 77

   Chapter 7 — *Always Be Connecting Diverse Dots* 84

Chapter 8 — *Discover This Secret Treasure Of Diverse Dots* 95

Section # 4 - Unleash your creative genius
.... 102

Chapter 9 — *Break The Invisible Wall Around Creativity* 103

Chapter 10 — *Change Your Question, Challenge Your Realities* 118

Chapter 11 — *Change Your Frame, Change Your Game* 130

Section # 5 - Your Subconscious Mind .. 143

Chapter 12 — *Where Do Wow Ideas Come From?* 144

Chapter 13 — *Let The Magic Begin* 153

Chapter 14 — *Make The Subconscious Mind Your Powerful Ally* 163

Chapter 15 — *Serendipity: Revel In Happy Accidents* 179

Chapter 16 – *Generating Ideas On Demand* 190

Chapter 17 – *Boost Your Creativity With Constraints* 192

Chapter 18 — *Become the Idea Machine* 202

Section # 7 - From Comfort Zone To 10x Zone 217

Chapter 19 — *From Comfort Zone To 10x Zone* 218

Answers 228
May I ask you for a small favor? 230

Preface

Each one of us is born creative.

And then one day, we went to school.

Our formal education began with formally muzzling our creativity. By the time we completed our education, the process of *'de-creativization'* was complete. The whole process is so effective that whenever we come across creative people, we consider them as gifted individuals. The reality is that all of us were as gifted as the creative ones. The only difference is, somehow, they managed to survive the *'de-creativizing'* effect of formal education.

"Every child is an artist. The problem is how to remain an artist once he grows up."

Pablo Picasso

I was no different. I was blissfully unaware, leading a perfectly uncreative life. Then a jolt came in the form of a most unexpected promotion in my corporate career.

Let me explain.

I started my career as a medical representative. But somewhere deep inside, I believed that the right place for me was in marketing. But I had neither the qualification nor the required experience. Hence, I focused on my sales career, rose to a managerial position, and continued to move up in my career ladder. Meanwhile, I also added a management qualification. Again, the thought of moving into marketing came to me, but by then, I had already moved up the ladder as a line manager. I thought shifting to marketing would mean starting from scratch, at the lowest marketing position. At that time, I didn't want to let go of my hard-earned middle management position. Besides, I was performing well and already expecting my next promotion.

Soon, the promotion happened. But it came with a big surprise. I was promoted to marketing manager without any prior marketing experience. It was like a dream come true!

Those were the days when FMCG ad agencies had not yet entered the pharmaceutical arena. Hence, to be a successful pharma marketer, creativity was a mandatory prerequisite. As a marketing head, I had a bright team of brand managers who expected me to help them provide creative, differentiating ideas. Not just my team, but my seniors too had high expectations from me. With the pressure of such high expectations, I could think of only mediocre, run-of-the-mill ideas.

My reputation was at stake.

I had only two choices — be creative or be regarded as a failure in my new role as a marketer. I opted for the first one.

Once I made the decision, I chased creativity with an intense focus. I searched and consumed every word I came across on the subject of creativity and innovation and tried to apply it to my day-to-day work. Regardless of the quality of ideas, I focussed on churning out ideas every single day. Initially, the results were pathetic. Fortunately, I had no choice but to keep trying. Gradually, the quality of ideas started improving. In the process, I learned the art of connecting dots. My ideas started getting better. Even others began to notice the difference.

I had crossed the first barrier.

At some point during my struggle, I discovered the powerful art of asking questions. (The topic of questions has been covered in this eBook). Asking questions is such a powerful process that it took my idea-generating ability to the next orbit.

Finally, the real breakthrough came when I learned to identify and challenge the hidden assumptions that stop everyone from getting breakthrough ideas. (There is a lot of interesting stuff on shattering assumptions that awaits you in this book.)

Fast forward to today. Since 2008, my creative agency helps pharmaceutical companies build big brands. I also offer strategic consulting to organizations looking for innovative ideas to stay ahead of the competition.

Today, my sole source of livelihood is strategy, marketing, creativity, and innovation.

This book has anecdotes, stories about great minds, case studies, scientific evidence, and many powerful techniques and exercises. Besides, I have put 20 years of my first-hand experience and learning into it. All this is to help you generate Ideas on Demand, which is the promise of this book.

Let's get started!

Section # 1 - Introduction

Creativity – Your long lever for 10x impact

"10x is easier than 10 percent."

– Astro Teller, Caption of Moonshots, CEO of X, formerly known as Google X

Way back in 2013, I read the above statement in *Wired* magazine[1]. At first glance, it sounded counterintuitive. I was intrigued and excited at the same time. Even when you think deeply about it, you will begin to understand how profound it is.

The article reads, *"Because when you're working to make things 10 percent better, you inevitably focus on the existing tools and assumptions, and on building on top of an existing solution that many people have already spent a lot of time thinking about. Such incremental progress is driven by extra effort, extra money, and extra resources."*

How do the people who get 10x results approach things differently?

I will answer it by borrowing an analogy from the life of Archimedes -- You get 10x results by using a lever that is long enough.

In the king's court, Archimedes was a well-respected figure. On many occasions, the king used to depend upon the scientific acumen of Archimedes to find out the answers to

seemingly impossible challenges. No wonder, whenever Archimedes proclaimed something, howsoever audacious it may sound, people knew that Archimedes would surely find ways to prove it, hence, learned to listen to him with due respect.

One day, in front of many people, Archimedes claimed that he could move the earth. Now, this was more than yet another audacious proclamation from Archimedes. It was too far-fetched even for Archimedes's standard. People knew for sure that this is something beyond even the great Archimedes. However, such was the reputation of Archimedes that no one could challenge him on his face. Nevertheless, it became the news of the town spread in hushed voices. Eventually, the murmur reached the king's ear. Even the king was surprised and somewhat annoyed.

The king summoned Archimedes to the court. "I heard you claim that you can move the earth, is it true?" the king demanded.

"Yes, your majesty, what you heard is correct," replied Archimedes pretending to be respectful.

"Can you demonstrate it?" With this question, the king knew that all Archimedes's pretensions would fall apart.

This was the very moment that Archimedes said something that would be remembered for centuries.

"Give me the lever long enough and a place to stand, and I can move the earth."

This was Archimedes's dramatic way of presenting the importance of the lever to the world. I often use this metaphor of long levers to describe those few things that fetch us disproportionate results.

Creativity is one such long lever, which you can use to create a 10x impact.

The most critical skill required today to propel innovation is creativity. Even in the 2010 IBM survey, 1,500 CEOs worldwide identified creativity as the single most important competency.

"Ideas are the currency of new economy."

– Richard Florida

Creativity is in demand like never before.

But what about the supply?

On the supply side, it tells a different story. As per the 2012 Adobe study findings, 80% of people felt that unlocking creativity is critical to economic growth. But at the same time, 75% of them admitted that they were under pressure to be productive rather than creative at work.

Give yourself an unfair advantage.

Mastering creativity will put you among the top 1% who can generate creative ideas at will. This will give you a massive competitive advantage.

With creativity and innovation under your belt, you will no longer be stuck with incremental results.

Get ready for exponential results.

If creativity is not one of your core strengths, I have only one suggestion to make. Drop everything. It's time to move on to the big game. Nothing can be more rewarding than being creative. In the case of other competencies, as you get better with them, your results improve incrementally. But getting better with creativity and innovation can change your results exponentially.

How will this book help you to unleash your creativity?

This book is not *about* creativity. This book is designed *to make you creative.* The whole book is structured keeping this single objective in mind. Before I explain the structure of this book, I want to share some research findings with you.

Creative brains are wired differently

Research published in [Proceedings of the National Academy of Sciences](#) stated that the brains of creative people are wired differently than most.[1]

In creative people, three brain networks, the default mode network, the executive network, and the salience network, are simultaneously activated.

This phenomenon in creative people, according to researchers, was quite unusual.

Why did researchers think that it was an unusual phenomenon? To understand it, we need to know the functionality of each of the networks.

When people are engaged in spontaneous thinking, such as mind-wandering, daydreaming, and imagining, **the default mode network** gets activated.

When people focus on their thought processes and evaluate the ideas, **the executive control network** gets activated.

When the executive control network is activated, the default network is deactivated.

This is how it usually works for most people.

In the case of creative people, activation of **the salience network** makes all the difference. The salience network operates as a switching mechanism between the default and executive networks.

This network plays a key role in alternating between idea generation and idea evaluation. In other words, an activated salience network ensures that the default mode network and the executive control network get simultaneously activated.

Roger Beaty, a postdoctoral fellow in Psychology and the first author of the study, concluded, *"What this shows is that the creative brain is wired differently. People who are more creative can simultaneously engage brain networks that **don't typically work together**."* He further added, "People who think **more flexibly** and come up with more creative ideas are better able to engage these networks that don't typically work together and bring these systems online."

Creativity and neuroplasticity

So, the research carried out by neuroscientists has proven that the brain of a creative thinker is wired differently.

What does this discovery mean to you?

Does it mean that you can't become a creative person?

No.

Here, neuroscientists have some good news for you – **neuroplasticity**.

Neuroplasticity is the ability of human brains to make new neural connections and make structural changes. For a long time, it was believed that neuroplasticity happens only in the case of children, and the brain of adults remains unchanged. However, thanks to research in neuroplasticity, it is now proven that even an adult's brain can be rewired.

Recent studies in neuroplasticity confirm that with divergent thinking exercises, your brain can be rewired similar to that of creative ones.

This study confirms the fact that creativity is not an inborn trait. Instead, it's like any other skill that can be acquired through training and exercise.

Just like any new skill, training your brain to think creatively takes time. But the more you exercise your brain, the more creative muscle you'll build.

At the same time, you need to understand that building your creativity muscle requires a systematic approach. If you want to build your physical muscles, do you go to the gym, randomly pick up any weight and start exercising? No. You follow a systematic plan laid down by your expert gym instructor. The same applies to building your creative muscles.

Keeping this in mind, I have structured this book so that even if you are a complete beginner, its step-by-approach approach will make you an idea machine.

Does it sound like a tall promise? Let me explain to you how this book is structured.

How is this book structured?

If I have to explain creativity in a single line, I would say creativity is all about connecting the dots and creating a wow. Hence, this topic is at the core of the book.

Section 1 of the book is the introduction, which you are reading now. It will set the context and the expectations and tell you how this book is designed to meet those expectations.

If you are still wondering whether you need this book, I will shortly share who this book is for. In that section, I have described different types of people who need this book. You can check out whether you can relate to any one of them.

Coming to **Section 2,** although I have said that connecting the dots is at the core of this book, straightway jumping to connecting the dots could be an overwhelming experience. This is because certain creativity blocks will make it nearly impossible for you. Learning to connect the different dots effortlessly requires rewiring your brain. But our experience, beliefs, and mental blocks harden our brain. Unless it is softened and made flexible, it can't be rewired. This is one primary reason why most people struggle to think creatively. In this section, you will understand and remove your creativity block. This will bring flexibility to your thinking. By the time you complete reading the section and do a few of the exercises given, you would notice a considerable shift in your thinking.

Once it is done, you will be ready for **Section 3**, which is about **connecting the dots**. "Connecting the dots" is an overused term. Many talk about it, but very few know how to do it.

What about you? Do you struggle to think of completely different, wow ideas?

This is because most people connect the same dots as others do and, therefore, get the same run-of-the-mill ideas.

Creativity involves bringing out wow ideas by connecting the dots the way no one ever has. But it is easier said than done. But not anymore. In this section, you will learn some powerful techniques to connect different dots.

Using some examples, I will hand-hold you through the entire process.

This is the stage when you will begin to generate some creative sparks that will surprise you and the people around you.

But you are still a step away from 'breakthrough' ideas. For that, you need to unshackle your creativity completely.

This is what you are going to do in **Section 4**.

Have you ever wondered how innovators, inventors, and creative geniuses are consistently able to bring forth breakthrough ideas?

Perhaps you thought that they are born geniuses.

The truth is that there stands an imaginary wall of assumptions between us and breakthrough ideas. Creative people not only can see it, but they also know how to break it.

In this section, you will learn powerful techniques with which you will be able to break the **biggest barrier of creativity**. In this section, you will be introduced to the secret that will help you unleash your creative genius. The secret key is **questions**. Creative people ask different questions that make all the difference. Here, you will learn the exact way to ask different questions to get **out-of-the-box ideas**.

Once it is done, your thinking process will transform. You will find yourself thinking of so many possibilities in seemingly impossible situations.

Section 5 is where the magic begins!

You might have heard about *Eureka moments.* Also, you might have read stories about some of the great scientific discoveries happening while seeing the dreams. Some inventions have happened accidentally.

Are such moments of epiphany reserved only for a select few?

Most importantly, where do all these wow ideas come from?

With the help of some solid research findings, you will understand what exactly happens in the brain during the process of generating wow ideas. I will share many examples and real-life stories behind the inventions to help you understand how your **subconscious mind** plays a critical role in getting those wow ideas. You will also learn different ways to train your subconscious mind to flood you with ideas.

You are still one step away from being officially known as an 'idea person.' 🙂

In **Section 6,** you will learn how, contrary to popular belief, you can use constraints to force the ideas out of your head.

Throughout this book, I have given exercises to help you build your creativity muscle at every appropriate stage.

Finally, in this section, your creativity muscle will be put through an ultimate challenge.

Once you complete it successfully, you will likely to be rebranded by the world as 'creative', and you will start thinking like one. In the process, you will master the skill of effortlessly generating **Ideas on Demand.**

Finally, **Section 7**. It's about taking bold action.

Ideas are of no value unless acted upon. Creativity, without action, is just a hobby. It may seem like a no-brainer, but in reality, most are too scared to present their ideas in front of the world due to the fear of rejection.

As said by Les Brown, *"The wealthiest place on the planet is the graveyard, because in the graveyard we will find inventions that we were never ever exposed to, ideas, dreams that never became a reality, hopes and aspirations that were never acted upon."*

Nothing can be more tragic than the great ideas not acted upon for want of courage.

This section will create a strong desire in you to leap from a comfort zone to a **10x zone**. You will learn the ways to overcome your fear.

This is when you will become truly **unstoppable**.

Sounds exciting? But before we move into the next topic, I have something important to say. It's about **exercises**.

Creativity is a skill, which is different from knowledge. For knowledge, you just need to read or listen and understand the subject. Whereas in the case of skill, you need to understand and practice. Therefore, creativity, like any other skill, requires practice. Hence, the exercises at the end of the chapters are crucial. A great deal of thought has gone into it. Therefore, I would urge you to attempt all of them seriously. You may be the type who likes to first complete reading the whole book uninterruptedly. In that case, you can first finish reading the book and then use the exercise section as a workbook, starting from the first chapter.

James Altucher recommends writing ten ideas daily. It's quite a powerful suggestion. From what I have gathered, many people, including James himself, immensely benefited by practicing it. But for this book's exercises, we will be following a somewhat different path.

1. The exercises given below the chapter are specific to your learning from that chapter.
2. The initial few exercises will help you understand your present level of ideation. It will be your starting point.
3. As you keep on attempting more exercises, you will notice a change in your ability to ideate. At some stage, you will comfortably cross the number ten. However, I don't want you to stop at that stage. After that, asking you to think of ten ideas would mean stopping your progress.
4. At the right stage, you will be introduced to a few powerful techniques with which you will be able to increase the ideas exponentially. By doing the exercises given at the end of that section, you will not just generate ten ideas but 10x ideas.
5. As you keep attempting these exercises, you will see a clear improvement in your idea-generating ability. Your self-belief will start changing.
6. Towards the end, you will be introduced to an ultimate challenge. After successfully completing your ultimate

challenge, there will be a complete shift in your self-belief.

That said, I strongly recommend you to read the book _Become an Idea Machine: Because Ideas Are the Currency of the 21st Century_ by Claudia Azula Altucher. The best part of this book is that it will guide you to write ten ideas a day for 365 days. When you do it, your brain would be completely rewired.

Is creativity all about problem-solving?

When Alan Barker told the MD of a successful training organization that he intended to write a book on creativity for managers, he replied: "They aren't interested in creativity. They want to know how to run their companies better."

This conversation happened way back in the nineties. Since then, things have changed a lot, if not drastically.

The corporate world no longer considers creativity a trait that belongs only to that weird tribe of artists, poets, sculptures, etc.

Creativity for problem-solving is surely one area that many organizations have embraced. But even today, in the corporate world, creativity is just a useful tool for problem-solving in the mind of many.

But is creativity all about problem-solving? I believe problem-solving is just one aspect of what creativity can achieve. Most people still fail to see the role of creativity in "opportunity-creating."

I prefer to use the word "challenge" rather than the "problem." There are two reasons for the same. First, by repeatedly referring to a given situation as a problem, I don't want to reinforce the belief that creativity is just for problem-solving. Second, problem as a word is emotionally associated with a negative connotation. In contrast, the word challenge brings out the best of you. This is how I look at it. Everyone may not have the same viewpoint. However, in this book, you are going to get used to the word "challenge."

Who is this book for?

A short answer – For everyone.

Creativity is no more a "nice to have" trait. In the 21st century, it has shifted to a "must-have" competence for individuals and organizations.

A long answer – Have a look at the list given below. Do any of the following challenges resonate with you? If your answer is 'yes' for one or more of the listed challenges, then continue reading. I assure you will read and even think of many striking ideas in this book. Keep your pen and notepad handy. You want to be taking notes of them all.

Do you feel stuck? To free yourself from a stuck situation, you first need more dots. Connecting them in different ways will create multiple options for you. This book will show you how to create many dots in every situation and create multiple possibilities connecting them creatively.

As a leader, do you wish to bring out innovative, breakthrough thinking in your team? You already know the idea that the leader's job is to offer solutions is rapidly becoming redundant. True leaders challenge their team to think of innovative ideas. This book will help you hone your skill of asking insightful questions that will bring out the best innovation from your team.

As an entrepreneur, do you still find yourself miles away from the business goals you had set for yourself? Are you working really hard but still unable to scale your business? Perhaps you are struggling to generate powerful ideas. You need to begin with lots of fresh ideas in order to zero down on the best ones. This book will show you to generate lots of ideas at will.

Do you feel that the lack of creativity is hurting your corporate career growth? Once you master the techniques of generating creative ideas, you will see yourself emerging as the go-to person for all the creative challenges that your organization faces.

Do you aspire to be an entrepreneur and pursue the areas where your passion lies but cannot figure out the way? You need to connect the right dots. That's what creative ones do. Once you learn to ask the right questions, you will create more dots around the area of your passion and learn to connect them into an exciting business model.

As a marketer, do you struggle to differentiate your brand? Perhaps you are stuck in a single frame. This book will encourage you to think in multiple frames. You will be able to make your brand stand out even in the undifferentiated market.

As an author, would you like to stand out from the rest by carving out a place, but at present, find your book buried under thousands of similar ones? Creativity is the answer. Once you master the techniques given in this book, you will find yourself thinking of fresh ideas that you can apply to writing, positioning, and successfully marketing your books.

Do you strongly believe that you have not done justice to the potential that you possess? Congratulations! You are among the select few who believe in their potential. You just need few creative tweaks to be able to live a life full of your potential

Do you believe that there are many opportunities around but can't figure out how to tap them? Again, congratulations! You are carrying the right belief. Technology has broken the barriers like place, expertise, resources and created a level field for everyone. Never before in history has there been so much opportunity for anyone residing in any part of the world. Techniques given in this book will help you to create a flood of opportunity in **any** situation.

Do you work in any one of those areas that demand a high degree of creativity? Once you finish reading this book, do the exercises given at the end of every chapter and consciously start putting your newly acquired skill in place, you will soon earn the reputation of being an idea machine.

Exercises

What is your biggest aspiration?

It is something that you aspire to be or achieve but are still not sure whether it can happen? In other words, you have still not stated it as your goal. Now it's time to do it.

Can you make it even bigger? Go ahead. Keep on increasing it till you reach a stage where you feel that it is no more doable. Stop at this stage.

The next step is to write it down as your most important goal. Be specific, give numbers to your aspirations.

Ask yourself, what stopped you from making it even bigger. List the challenges that will keep you from achieving the same. Write them down, clearly defining every challenge.

The next step is the possible solutions that you could think of to crack all these challenges. Please write them down if there aren't many.

Now, you have your goal, the list of challenges, and possible ways to crack these challenges.

What if you could find solutions for all the stated challenges? Will your goal remain the same? Perhaps, in such a scenario, you can achieve something even bigger. We shall call it the possible scenario. Please write it down. I know you may not fully believe it. But still write it down, again with the revised numbers.

Now you have a document in which you have written the above instructions under the four headings.

1. Your most important goal.
2. The list of well-defined challenges.
3. Possible solutions that you could think of.
4. Your revised goal (in the best possible scenario).

Great!

Now approach the remaining content of this book with the hundred percent commitment to make it happen.

Let's together begin this exciting journey.

Introduction - References

1. https://www.wired.com/2013/02/moonshots-matter-heres-how-to-make-them-happen/
2. https://www.ibm.com/downloads/cas/1VZV5X8J
3. https://news.adobe.com/news/news-details/2012/Study-Reveals-Global-Creativity-Gap/default.aspx
4. https://www.pnas.org/content/115/5/1087
5. https://www.amazon.com/Become-Idea-Machine-Because-Currency-ebook/dp/B00S1PRTL4/ref=tmm_kin_swatch_0?_encoding=UTF8&qid=&sr=
6. https://www.amazon.com/Creativity-Managers-Alan-Barker/dp/8174460780/ref=sr_1_1?dchild=1&keywords=creativity+for+managers&qid=1622303594&s=books&sr=1-1

Section # 2 - Removing Creativity Blocks

Chapter 1 — *Creativity Is Not My Cup Of Tea*

Creativity Block # 1 – Lack of self-belief

Whenever the topic of creativity comes up during a discussion, the most common expression that I hear is, "Creativity is not my cup of tea."

Every time I hear this, I probe further, "Why do you think so?"

In response, I hear something like this – "Because I have tried on several occasions to come up with some wow ideas. But what I produced each time was a pile of garbage."

Does this resonate with you? Do you judge yourself as a non-creative being based on your experience with idea generation?

If your answer is 'yes', then I am afraid you are making a big mistake.

Before I explain why, let me share an interesting story from the book *Art & Fear* by David Bayles and Ted Orland[1].

"The ceramics teacher announced on opening day that he was dividing the class into two groups. All those on the left side of the studio, he said, would be graded solely on the quantity of work they produced, all those on the right solely on its quality.

His procedure was simple: on the final day of class, he would bring in his bathroom scales and weigh the work of the "quantity" group: fifty pounds of pots rated an "A", forty pounds a "B", and so on. Those being graded on "quality", however, needed to produce only one pot – albeit a perfect one – to get an "A".

Well, came grading time and a curious fact emerged: the works of highest quality were all produced by the group being graded for quantity. It seems that while the "quantity" group was busily churning out piles of work – and learning from their mistakes – the "quality" group had sat theorizing about perfection, and in the end, had little more to show for their efforts than grandiose theories and a pile of dead clay."

Do you get the point? The group that eventually produced the highest quality of pots must have started with horrible ones. Regardless, they continued producing more pots. Eventually, they ended up producing a perfect one.

Similarly, in your case, you need to accept that your initial ideas will be garbage. Learn to be comfortable with your daily pile of garbage. Commit yourself to produce it every day. In the process, you will achieve something priceless – you will rewire your brain the way it is wired in creative people.

Don't form a self-limiting belief that you are not creative based on the quality of your present or past ideas.

I have shared the scientific evidence from studies in neuroplasticity to convince you that creativity is a skill, like any other skill, that can be acquired. But as long as you keep believing that you are not creative, it will be impossible for you to acquire it.

As Henry Ford has famously quoted, "Whether you think you can, or you think you can't – you're right."

Our core beliefs about ourselves get deeply rooted in our subconscious mind. Our subconscious mind ensures that they become our reality.

In Section 5, you will understand the amazing power of your subconscious mind. You will also learn to use some powerful affirmations to shift your belief. In the same section, I will share some solid techniques to make it your trusted ally in helping you generate ideas on demand.

I know one thing for sure: if you commit yourself one hundred percent to become a creative person, consume the content of this book and practice all the exercises, you will notice the change. Once that happens, your belief will automatically change. But the tough part is committing yourself one hundred percent while believing deep within that you are not a creative person.

Here is a practical approach that will work for you — Till the time you complete reading this book, keep aside your belief of you not being a creative type of person. If you do it, you will be doing yourself a great favor.

Exercises

1

You, the happiness experts

Many people live their life trying to find out how to BE happy. There are even more people who wait for the perfect future that they believe will make them happy.

"Happiness is not something you postpone for the future; it is something you design for the present."

- Jim Rohn

Imagine that you are a happiness expert. As an expert, you say quite often, "Happiness lies in being happy NOW, without changing a thing."

You have received a request from a famous publication to share practical tips on "Being happy in every present moment, without changing a thing."

What are the tips you will give?

This is your first ideation exercise. Please think of as many ideas as you can. You are not allowed to refer to the internet, books, or any other source. You have to think of suggestions from your knowledge and experience. Remember the ceramics class story? Every suggestion need not be world-class. Focus on the quantity. A detailed description is not needed. Just bullet points will do. Please remember to number it.

How many suggestions could you think of?

2

How many ways can you use a brick?

Please think of all the possible ways one can use a brick. Again, write them down with numbering.

What is your final number?

References

https://www.amazon.com/Art-Fear-Observations-Rewards-Artmaking-ebook-dp-B0042JSQLU/dp/B0042JSQLU/ref=mt_other?_encoding=UTF8&me=&qid=1624908427

https://www.amazon.com/Art-Fear-Observations-Rewards-Artmaking-ebook/dp/B0042JSQLU/ref=tmm_kin_swatch_0?_encoding=UTF8&qid=&sr=

Chapter 2 — *"Don't Ask Stupid Questions"*

Creativity Block # 2 – <u>Fear of sounding stupid</u>

Who asks a lot of stupid questions?

Children.

And who are the most creative?

Of course, children.

In the 1960s, Dr. George Land, a creative performance researcher, did a study in which he tested the divergent thinking ability of 1600 children. At the age of 5, 98 percent of children scored in the "highly creative range."

What do you think is the most striking aspect of children of that age? They ask lots of questions. A study done in the UK by online retailer *Littlewoods.com* revealed that children aged four ask an incredible 390 questions per day.

But as children start growing up, their 'cute' questions are frowned upon as stupid ones by their parents and relatives. They are admonished to "stop behaving like a kid."

The same story continues in school. Our education system rewards the right answer, never a good question.

The same study found that by the time the children asking an incredibly high number of questions at four years had reached the age of nine, the number of questions asked dropped to 37%.

So, what happens to creativity?

I had earlier spoken about the study conducted by Dr. Land on 1600 children to test their divergent thinking ability. However, that was only a part of the story. This study tracked the divergent thinking ability of 1600 children over 20 years. Here is the full story:

At the age of 5, 98 percent of children scored in the "highly creative range." After 5 years, only 30 percent scored in the highly creative range. By age 15, this number dropped to 12 percent. By the age of 25, their creative score got reduced to only 2 percent.

Please listen to Dr. George Land's Tedx talk. You will find it quite fascinating[1].

Once people move to the corporate world, they are anxious to sound intelligent. Hence, they want to avoid asking questions that may make them look stupid in the eyes of others.

But some people continue to ask childlike questions. These are among the best creative minds the world has ever produced. They are the ones who leave their mark on the world.

"What would it be like to race alongside a light beam?"

This was the question sixteen-year-old Einstein asked himself. That eventually led to the theory of relativity.

Einstein retained his childlike mind, filled with wonder.

In his book on Einstein, Walter Isaacson writes[2], *"Curiosity, in Einstein's case, came not just from a desire to question the mysterious. More importantly, it came from a childlike sense of marvel that propelled him to question the familiar, those concepts that, as he once said, 'the ordinary adult never bothers about.'"*

Bring the perspective of a child

One of the important steps of cracking the creative challenge is looking at the same challenge from a different perspective. This will help you in **reframing** the problem. There are many ways to bring a different perspective. You will learn about them in chapter 10.

One way of changing the perspective is by thinking like a child. So next time when you try to crack a challenge, ask yourself—how would a ten-year-old child look at this problem? You may, at times, be surprised to see that this approach brings out some obvious and, at the same time, critical aspects of the challenge you might have completely overlooked.

If you are like most, trying to avoid asking questions that will make you sound stupid, you are blocking breakthrough ideas. This is a creativity block that has to be busted.

"My greatest strength is to be ignorant and ask a few questions."

- Peter Drucker

Peter Drucker is regarded as the father of modern management. He had built his reputation over so many years. He never felt he was putting his reputation at stake by showing his ignorance by way of questions.

Why should you feel so?

We consider our initial briefing meeting with the client as an opportunity to ask every possible question. Mind you, all questions that we ask are not very intelligent sounding. Some of them may sound outrightly ignorant. We have learned that the more questions we ask, the more angles we will work upon. And the more the angles we work upon, the greater will be the wow. Clients will judge us on the quality of the ideas we will eventually bring to the table, not on the quality of the questions we ask.

There had been several instances when we were hesitant to ask few questions that may sound stupid. But we went ahead and asked. As a result, we got insights that we would have never known had we not asked those questions.

In chapter 10, we are going to cover the topic of questions in detail. Meanwhile, if you find yourself holding back a few questions during your next interaction because they may sound stupid, stop judging and start shooting (your questions 🙂). Watch how others react. Also, watch what extra knowledge or perspective you get by asking those questions.

Exercises

Okay, so asking stupid questions results in breakthrough ideas. What's next?

Start asking stupid questions? Make a list of ten stupid questions? Maybe one hundred?

It's tough. You need to do some preparatory work.

How are we conditioned to respond to stupidity?

We feel ashamed of stupid things done in the past. We keep them closely guarded with ourselves.

We can't stand any sort of stupidity. Some get annoyed, some ridicule it.

We feel scared of being seen speaking or acting stupidly.

The rewiring needs to happen in steps.

<u>Step 1</u>: Stop being too harsh with yourself for a few stupid things you have done in the past (and still do occasionally 🙂).

<u>Step 2</u>: Learn to be more tolerant of the stupid questions of others.

Step 3: Learn to be comfortable with asking stupid questions.

1

Share YOUR stupidity

Try to remember the most stupid things that you had done in the past. It could be during your childhood or last week. Share them with a minimum of three persons.

Observe your feelings...

How did you feel *while* sharing them with others?

How did you feel *after* sharing them with others?

Do you still feel ashamed of your past stupidity? After the exercise, if you feel a little lighter, keep continuing even after completing this book. You may think of more such instances and share them with more people.

2

Becoming tolerant to stupidity

Below are a few stupid questions (they will serve you as an example for the third exercise).

Your challenge is to think of some equally or more stupid answer(s) for each of these questions.

- If everyone starts appreciating stupid questions, what would smart people do?

- While doing a Google search, will I become lucky if I click on "I am feeling lucky"?
- Did you experience good luck after doing a Google search with "I am feeling lucky"?
- Why did Google remove the "I am feeling lucky" search option? Didn't they want people to feel lucky?
- He kept telling you about the elephant in the room. I didn't see any. Did you? If not, why didn't you tell him?
- If you found out the way to go back to your childhood days. But you are allowed to carry only one thing from today's world, what would that be?
- When the sun gets a fever, does it get even hotter?
- What if, before consuming, my fortune cookie falls and breaks, will it impact my fortune?
- Those who smell the rat, can they smell a cat too?
- If a cloud stores water, can it be stored in a container?
- You said, "I quit smoking cold turkey", but I never saw you smoking one?

3

Asking stupid questions

Now it's your turn to think of stupid questions

Think of five stupid questions. First, make a long list and select the five that you feel are the most stupid ones.

By doing these exercises, if you have started feeling somewhat stupid, don't worry. It won't *make* you stupid. Instead, you will become more creative.

References

1. https://www.youtube.com/watch?v=ZfKMq-rYtnc
2. https://www.amazon.com/gp/product/B007F5SFWS/ref=dbs_a_def_rt_bibl_vppi_i6

Chapter 3 — "First, I Want Complete Clarity"

Creativity Block # 3 – <u>Discomfort with ambiguity and uncertainty</u>

When we come to know something, and if it triggers our interest, our mind wants to know the answer that once and for all settles the matter. Until such time, unconsciously, our mind keeps asking questions.

Is it true or false?

What she did was right, or was it wrong on her part?

Between two opposing groups, whom I support?

Can you imagine your mind arriving at the answers that are something like, "Maybe right, maybe wrong," or "She is right as well as wrong." Settling with such answers would mean continuing to live in a state of ambiguity.

The human mind hates ambiguity. It always wants to be certain. People feel good, comfortable, and safe when they are clear about things to the minutest of details.

Unfortunately, that's not how life works. Instead of clarity, it presents us with a state of perfect chaos.

How do most people respond to complex and ambiguous challenges?

On many occasions, I have seen managers taking quick decisions and moving on to the next item on their agenda. They consider themselves as decisive leaders. But in reality, due to their lack of tolerance towards ambiguity, uncertainty, and anxiety to arrive at clarity, they tend to rush to the solution by choosing the best option among the available ones. On most occasions, such half-baked solutions are linear, uninteresting, and devoid of creativity.

Creative thinkers can live with ambiguity for a longer period

[An Egyptian study](#) published in 2020 involving 18 architecture students found a significant correlation between students' creative thinking abilities and their tolerance for ambiguity.[1]

"It's not that I'm so smart, it's just that I stay with problems longer."

- Einstein

Faced with a complex situation, creative people are more likely to come up with an out-of-the-box solution. They can stay with ambiguity for a longer period. Hence, they don't have the urge to rush to premature solutions. In fact, they often procrastinate taking any decision and work till the end to find breakthrough ideas, and more often than not, they do.

Adam Grant, a famous psychologist, influencer, and bestselling author, found that creative people are procrastinators. I strongly recommend you to listen to his interesting Ted Talk[2] - The surprising habit of original thinkers.

George Eastman's leap of faith in the world of ambiguity and uncertainty

Most people are unable to tolerate ambiguity. They want to be absolutely clear about how things would work. As a result, they don't act on creative ideas and let big opportunities slip out of their hands. But George Eastman was different. His "Eastman Dry Plate Company" was making a lot of profit marketing dry plates. But seeing the future opportunity, he moved to film. Later, while his company was dominating the black and white business, color films were invented. Even though the initial color photographs appear inferior to black and white film, seeing the future possibilities, Eastman was quick to invest in it.

Eastman's Kodak camera was truly a disruption at that time. It placed the power of photography in the hands of anyone who could press a button. It revolutionized photography in the true sense.

How Kodak lost its way

Nearly a century later, the top management of Eastman Kodak company did the exact opposite. They saw the advent of digital photography on the horizon. But they could not tolerate the ambiguity and uncertainty associated with it. They continued to cling to the certainty and security of their existing film business and refused to pursue digital technology, resulting in the company's downfall.

It may come as a surprise to many of you that way back in 1975, Kodak's engineer, Steven J. Sasson, invented the world's first self-contained (portable) digital camera. Sasson presented it to his bosses, but no one was impressed.

As [Sasson later told the New York Times](), *"it was filmless photography, so management's reaction was, 'that's cute — but don't tell anyone about it."*[3]

Accepting this invention of filmless photography and further acting on it would mean shaking all the pillars on which stood Kodak's highly profitable business model, which was referred to as Silver Halide.

This business model had given Kodak a virtual monopoly on the United States photography market and made money on every step of the photographic process. If someone wanted to photograph any event, he would likely use a Kodak Instamatic, Kodak film, and Kodak flash cubes. He would have it processed either at a shop or mailed the film to Kodak and get back prints made with Kodak chemicals on Kodak paper.

Kodak's management was not very enthusiastic about this invention of digital photography.

They were not willing to cannibalize their existing business model with high profitability and virtual monopoly over the market. Just to give you an idea, when Steve Sasson presented the digital camera to the management, Kodak commanded 90% of film sales and 85% of camera sales in the United States. Kodak chose to continue with the existing model that gave them a sense of certainty and security rather than pursuing the digital path that was unclear and ambiguous.

As consumer preference shifted from print to digital photography, Kodak steadily started losing its market share as well as profits. Finally, in 2012, Kodak filed for bankruptcy protection.

Kodak's creative ad campaigns were built around the need to preserve 'significant' occasions such as family events and holidays. These were referred to as 'Kodak moments', which became part of everyday life.

Kodak believed that 'Kodak moments' are going to stay forever. They somehow couldn't imagine the world without traditional film.

Today, in the business world, Kodak Moments are referred to as those moments when organizations lose big opportunities due to their insistence on clarity and intolerance to ambiguity.

Exercises

As we saw in this chapter, clarity involves concluding things with definitive "yes or no" or "right or wrong". Leaving it open brings ambiguity. These exercises are designed to help you become comfortable with ambiguity and also make you open to opposing viewpoints.

I guess you will enjoy it due to its sheer novelty. But if your brain is strongly wired for clarity and certainty, you may find it a little tough. Nevertheless, it will help you to make your brain more flexible.

1

Think of the topic that interests you the most. The topic should be something you have been thinking, studying, practicing in your life and, therefore, have a good deal of clarity on the subject. Identify a few keywords around that topic. Once you are done, take these keywords and head to Google. Type "quote" and your keyword, one at a time. You will see some of the great quotes that will resonate with your thinking. Pick up the one that resonates with you the most. Move away from the internet and return to the document or the word you are using for the exercise. Now think of the viewpoint that is completely opposing to your selected quote. Your challenge is to think of as many points as you can in support of the opposing viewpoint. One condition is you are not supposed to search the internet for the answers, but you need to think and generate them.

Finally, write down all the points.

2

Think of all the past and present presidents, prime ministers, or heads of state, whatever the constitutional leader is referred to as in your country. Whom do you dislike the most? In this exercise, you need to Google and try to understand the positive side of her or him. After you have studied enough pieces about that person, you need to write in your words (no copy-paste) a list of good or positive points about the person.

Some of you may say that there is nothing good about the leader you dislike the most. You KNOW it. Some of you may say that doing this exercise would mean going against the principles, values, beliefs, and positions you stand for. My response to you is, this is just an exercise. Please try it out. The exercise is not about the person, it is about you. By attempting it, your lifelong belief won't change, but the way you think will.

In both the above exercises, the starting point was hundred percent clarity and certainty. On both the topics, you had no doubt whatsoever. From that standpoint, when you shift your stand to, "This is true, but the opposite is also true" and "he is a rascal, but at times he is good too", you bring in ambiguity and uncertainty.

To what extent have you succeeded in achieving it?

References

1. https://www.researchgate.net/publication/340113299_The_relationship_between_tolerance_of_ambiguity_and_creativity_in_architectural_design_studio
2. https://www.ted.com/talks/adam_grant_the_surprising_habits_of_original_thinkers/transcript?language=en
3. https://www.nytimes.com/2008/05/02/technology/02kodak.html

Chapter 4 — "What's the right answer?"

Creativity Block # 4 – *The Right Answer Syndrome*

Imagine that the below Roman equation is created using movable sticks. It reads as, "11 plus 1 equals 10," which is obviously incorrect.

$$XI + I = X$$

Your challenge is to correct the equation by moving the least number of sticks without touching plus or equal signs. How many sticks do you need to move?

If your answer is one (one stick), I have two questions for you:

How much time did you take to arrive at the answer?

What did you do after you arrived at the answer?

Perhaps you are somewhat surprised by my second question. I will come back to it in a short while. Meanwhile, let me share with you an interesting anecdote.

Mulla Nasruddin became the judge of the town. One day two men came to Nasruddin for arbitration.

The plaintiff presented his case. He articulated his side very persuasively. Mulla Nasruddin appeared quite impressed with the argument. "You are right," said Mulla, nodding his head vehemently.

"Wait a minute," protested the defendant. "You haven't yet heard me. You can't express your opinion without doing so."

"You are right," said Nasruddin while nodding his head, "please go on."

The defendant articulated his case in an equally persuasive way. Mulla again appeared quite impressed. "You are right," said Mulla, nodding his head appreciatively.

The court clerk, who was watching the proceeding silently, couldn't take it anymore. He said to Mulla, "Sir, with due respect, I would like to point it out to you that these gentlemen are fighting on opposite grounds. Hence, they both can't be right."

Hearing these words from the clerk, Mulla Nasruddin nodded his head and said, "you are right."

Did you find the above anecdote quite funny? You have found it so because of your core belief that there is only one right answer in such a dispute.

We live in a world that is conditioned to *The Right Answer* way of thinking. The mind of creative people is wired differently. They can effortlessly think of many right answers to any given challenge.

Mulla Nasruddin was different, a creative type. For him, it was perfectly natural to have more right answers to any given situation.

"The test of a first-rate intelligence is the ability to hold two opposed ideas in mind at the same time and still retain the ability to function."

- F. Scott Fitzgerald

Let me come back to the incorrect equation that I asked you to correct.

By asking you what you did after arriving at the answer, I wanted to determine whether you continued to look for more-right answers.

If your answer is 'no', then ask yourself—why didn't I think of exploring more-right answers?

I can hear you asking me, "Having arrived at the right answer, where is the need to look for more-right answers?"

If you are solving a math paper, then there is no need. But for improving your creativity, there is every need to look for more right answers.

By the way, if you recall the question, I had asked you to move "the least number of sticks." Don't you think zero is the least number, not one?

Surprised?

If your answer was one, let me tell you something. There are at least three ways to correct the equation without touching any stick. But you stopped at your first answer, thinking it to be *the* right one.

Give it a try one more time. If you cannot think of all the three ways, you can find the answers at the end of this book.

The Right Answer Syndrome

Our brain is wired to look for the right answer, and once it finds one, it stops looking beyond. This is known as *The Right Answer Syndrome.*

The same holds good with the ideation. After the initial struggle, once we think of a good idea, we stop looking for more. What do you normally do? After you find a great idea, do you keep looking for more wow ideas? If you don't, you have to consciously work on *The Right Answer Syndrome* to rewire your brain, else it will block your creativity.

"Nothing is more dangerous than an idea when it is the only one you have."

- Emile Chartier Alain

Let me share with you another fascinating anecdote.

This story is about a question in a physics exam at the University of Copenhagen. The story goes like this:

"Describe how to determine the height of a skyscraper with a barometer."

One student replied: "You tie a long piece of string to the neck of the barometer, then lower the barometer from the roof of the skyscraper to the ground. The length of the string plus the length of the barometer will equal the height of the building."

This highly original answer so incensed the examiner that the student was failed immediately. The student appealed on the grounds that his answer was indisputably correct, and the university appointed an independent arbiter to decide the case.

The arbiter judged that the answer was indeed correct but did not display any noticeable knowledge of physics. To resolve the problem, it was decided to call the student in and allow him six minutes to provide a verbal answer that showed at least a minimal familiarity with the basic principles of physics.

For five minutes, the student sat in silence, forehead creased in thought.

The arbiter reminded him that time was running out, to which the student replied that he had several extremely relevant answers but couldn't make up his mind which to use. On being advised to hurry up, the student replied as follows:

"Firstly, you could take the barometer up to the roof of the skyscraper, drop it over the edge, and measure the time it takes to reach the ground. The height of the building can then be worked out from the formula H = 0.5g x t squared. But bad luck on the barometer. Or, if the sun is shining, you could measure the height of the barometer, then set it on one end and measure the length of its shadow. Then you measure the length of the skyscraper's shadow, and thereafter, it is a simple matter of proportional arithmetic to work out the skyscraper's height. But if you wanted to be highly scientific about it, you could tie a short piece of string to the barometer and swing it like a pendulum, first at ground level and then on the roof of the skyscraper. The height is worked out by the difference in the gravitational restoring force T = 2 pi sq root (l/g)."

"...or if the skyscraper has an outside emergency staircase, it would be easier to walk up and mark off the height of the skyscraper in barometer lengths, then add them up. If you merely wanted to be boring and orthodox about it, of course, you could use the barometer to measure the air pressure on the roof of the skyscraper and the ground and convert the difference in millibars into feet to give the height of the building."

"But since we are constantly being exhorted to exercise independence of mind and apply scientific methods, undoubtedly the best way would be to knock on the janitor's door and say to him, 'If you would like a nice new barometer, I will give you this one if you tell me the height of this skyscraper'."

The student was Niels Bohr, who was known for proposing the model of the atom wherein the electrons were much like the planets in our solar system orbiting around the nucleus. Niels Bohr went on to win the Nobel Prize for Physics.

I came across this story on social media. I don't know if the above incident actually happened. But it's a good anecdote that helps us understand how creative people who are differently wired never stop at the first right answer.

Now, coming back to *The Right Answer Syndrome*.

Why does the human mind always look for *The Right Answer*?

There are two reasons.

The first reason starts with our upbringing. As I said earlier, we are brought up in *The Right Answer* society. As a child, you learned that 'an acceptable' right answer is appreciated and rewarded. But many other answers that are high on imagination are not. This learning gets reinforced as you go to school. You quickly learn that you score marks only when you give an answer expected by the teacher.

You also get conditioned to multiple-choice questions, wherein you are supposed to choose the right answer from the four options given. Once you check the box corresponding to the right answer, what happens to the remaining ones? Of course, they all are wrong!

By the time you complete your studies, the mold of *The Right Answer* is permanently formed. As an adult, for every situation or challenge, you keep searching for the right answer. And the moment you find one, you stop looking for more answers because you have learned that the remaining ones are obviously wrong once you find the right one.

The second reason I have already discussed in the previous section – low threshold towards ambiguity, uncertainty, and paradoxes. Whenever we are confronted with such situations, we try to bring clarity as fast as possible by quickly finding the right answer.

To overcome this creativity block, you will be required to do a lot of unlearning. First, you need to let go of your strongly held *The Right Answer* Syndrome. Next time, when you think you have found *the* right answer, continue looking for more-right answers. Eventually, you need to develop a new mind that can live in peace with multiple ideas, even if some of them could even be conflicting with each other. You need to apply the same unlearning process even during the idea generation stage.

*"**Most people stop looking when they find the proverbial needle in the haystack. I would continue looking to see if there were other needles.**"*

- Einstein

When you shift your mindset from *The Right Answer* to *Many Right Answers*, you open the door to a flow of creative ideas. You will notice a big change in your creative ability. Whenever a creative idea flashes, you will remind yourself not to get married with the first best ideas. As you will know that even better ideas are on the way.

This is what we do as a part of our agency work. We have no choice. Our clients come to us when they are not able to go beyond the first good idea. And they pay us to present to them many wow ideas. During brainstorming sessions, when we are working on projects for different clients. During our brainstorming on a complex challenge, after the initial struggle, suddenly a wow idea flashes. What's next? We simply park it and start exploring a different angle. We continue till we get at least four wow ideas.

Okay, how would you get started? Start with a simple math problem given in the exercise.

Exercises

This exercise is intended to rewire your brain to develop the habit of looking for the more-right answers.

What is half of thirteen?

Is your answer 6.5? That's the first right answer.

Now, your challenge is to find out the more-right answers.

You can find the answers at the end of the book.

Chapter 5 — *"Be practical"*

Creativity Block # 5 – <u>Being judgmental</u>

You might have heard about how bosses or organizations kill creative ideas. But do you know? The majority of creative ideas get killed by someone even before they are presented to a larger group. And that someone is you.

We tend to get too critical or judgmental with our own creative ideas. As a result, most of them don't even see the light of the day. If you critically judge the ideas too early, you may end up throwing some unpolished diamonds out of the window, believing them to be ordinary stones.

Ideas are born ugly

At the initial stage of our new assignment, I often jokingly tell my colleagues that the client will be shocked if he happens to see our work now.

In the beginning, our work looks messy, ideas sound horrible, but we are not worried because we have learned two things —**1.** Ideas are born ugly. **2.** Some ideas will eventually connect with other ideas.

Hence, instead of judging them too critically, we try to nurture them and allow them to develop further.

1. Thou shalt not judge

Ed Catmull puts it quite candidly about Pixar movies in his book, _Creativity Inc_, *"Early on, all of our movies suck."* He further adds that it is our job to take them *"from suck to non-suck."*

All of you are familiar with the word brainstorming. "Let's brainstorm" is the common lingo used in corporates whenever a group of people wants to ideate on something.

Way back in 1939, Alex F. Osborn developed a structured method called brainstorming. In his method, he laid down certain rules. One rule is "defer judgment". As per the rule, participants are not allowed to judge the ideas shared by others. Osborn believed that suspending the judgment takes away any kind of inhibition from the mind of the participants.

On this count, I am in full agreement with Osborn. But what happens when you are ideating alone?

Many people tend to forget that while ideating alone, the same principle holds good. If you are at an initial stage of learning creativity, simultaneously ideating and judging will retard your progress. During the **initial stage of ideation**, follow these two commandments— 1. You will not judge (any idea) 2. You will not discard (any idea)

2. Thou shalt not discard

Most of the time, stand-alone ideas may not sound great, but cross-pollination or fusion with other ideas brings the magic. This is why you should not discard any ideas at the initial stage. We are going to discuss it at length in the section, Connecting the Dots.

It is important to understand why we tend to judge our ideas too harshly and reject them. Here are some of the reasons why people do it. What is your reason? Being aware is half the job done.

It is not practical

Our world is full of people who want creative ideas but are unwilling to move out of their comfort zone. They keep churning "practical" or "feasible" ideas that are undifferentiated and devoid of any wow. Worse still, they reject some breakthrough ideas just because they don't sound practical.

Don't apply the measure of practicality to reject at least your own ideas in the beginning. At the idea generation stage, you need to focus on generating creative ideas. Only towards the end, you need to figure out ways to make it practical.

No one has ever thought of it

This can never be the reason to reject. On the contrary, congratulate yourself. You have thought of something that no one did. Such ideas should become part of your shortlisted list.

These are the ideas you would want to pursue further.

It sounds crazy

As your brain starts getting rewired due to continuous practice, you will notice a change in the quality of your ideas. Instead of the same run-of-the-mill 'practical' ideas, you will start getting ideas that are different, audacious with a tinge of craziness. You will find yourself quite excited. But the very next moment, self-doubts will start creeping in. You will find asking yourself questions like –

"If it is such a great idea, why has no one ever thought about it?"

"This sounds crazy."

"What if people laugh at my idea?"

This will bring to the surface one more block of creativity – 'Fear of Rejection'.

In Section 7, I am going to talk at length about this deep-rooted creativity block. Meanwhile, let me share a real story of someone who thought of one of the craziest ideas and took courageous action.

How a copywriter went on to become a millionaire with a crazy idea

In the summer of 1975, Gary Dahl was enjoying a drink with a bunch of his friends. The discussion turned to pets. Someone complained how hard it was to feed and look after them.

Dahl jokingly mentioned that one could have a rock as a perfect pet. As rock would not need to be fed, walked, bathed, or groomed, it would not die, become sick, or be disobedient.

Everyone had a hearty laugh, and the conversation ended. But not with Dahl. For him, it was one of those crazy ideas with a huge business opportunity. "Why not?" he wondered, "With my copywriting skill and a dash of humor, it can become a new craze."

He went ahead and launched the product called 'Pet Rock' and the craze it became! In six months, he sold around $6 million worth of pet rocks.

What made it a super hit brand was a 'training manual' that carried instructions on taking care of the pet rock.

Here is a glimpse of the 32-page training manual for Dahl's pet rock.

> **Taking care of your pet rock:**
> 1) **Swimming and bathing** - Never take your pet rock swimming. They are known to be poor swimmers and will sink to the bottom. It is ok to give them an occasional bath in shallow water.
> 2) **Feeding** – No one knows what pet rocks like to eat, but they seem to thrive without food. It is not necessary to feed your pet rock
> 3) **Exercise** – Pet rocks can be quite lazy. They do enjoy being tossed in the air sometimes, but should never be thrown at anything.
> 4) **Traveling** – Pet rocks enjoy going on vacations. They prefer traveling in pockets.
> 5) **Training** – Pet rocks are easy to train. They can quickly learn to "sit", "stay", and "play dead".
> However, they are also very stubborn and will not come when called.

Source: Wiki Commons

Don't let your crazy ideas scare you. This is what you should be aiming for. Crazy ideas are the ones that stand a very good chance of getting breakthrough results.

At a seminar, someone presented a crazy idea, and Niels Bohr, the renowned Danish physicist, said, *"We are all agreed that your theory is crazy. The question which divides us is whether it is crazy enough."*

Creative people find crazy and absurd ideas quite exciting.

Einstein had said, "If your ideas at first aren't absurd, there's no hope for them."

Exercise

We are going to revisit the bricks exercise. During your last attempt, I am sure you must have written all the ways of using bricks that you have seen. Did you invent a few more novel ways? How many? This is your second chance to add more ways to it.

This is the time to be imaginative, even if it is impractical, and yes, you can even think of some crazy ideas. Today for once, you will permit yourself to celebrate the craziness.

References

1. https://www.encyclopedia.com/history/culture-magazines/pet-rocks
2. https://en.wikipedia.org/wiki/Pet_Rock#:~:text=Pet%20Rock%20is%20a%20collectible,with%20straw%20and%20breathing%20holes.

Section # 3 - Connecting the Dots

Chapter 6 — *Creativity is all about connecting the dots*

For an idea to be creative, it must elicit a 'wow'. But a wow is not the only thing it needs. In order to be creative, ideas must add value, make a difference, enable progress, open the door of opportunities, and do many more things that bring fulfillment to our lives.

There is something more.

Your idea also needs to be original.

"Creativity is the process of having original ideas which have value."

— Ken Robinson

"Okay, I get it. Creativity is all about having original ideas," you are saying. "But isn't it something I already knew?"

Possibly, yes. Hold on till the next paragraph. My guess is that it says something you haven't heard.

Creative people steal ideas

Austin Kleon came to the limelight with his book[1] carrying a bold and provocative title — *[Steal Like an Artist.](#)*

He starts off his book with the following lines:

Every artist gets asked the question, "Where do you get your ideas?" The honest answer, "I steal them."

He is not alone. Many artists have said it much before, on similar lines.

"Art is theft."

- Pablo Picasso

"The only art I'll ever study is stuff I can steal from."

- David Bowie

"Stealing the ideas?" I hear you saying, "Didn't you share some other quote that states, creativity is all about having original ideas which have value?"

If you are confused with this contradiction and not feeling too happy about it, I urge you to get used to it. You are learning one more lesson in creativity, which is to master creativity. You must learn to be at peace with contradictions and paradoxes.

Now, let me come back to the question that might be bothering you a lot — How can one steal ideas and claim to be original at the same time?

The answer lies in the ***dots***.

What are dots?

Dots include everything that goes into the making of a new innovative idea. Dots could be past experience, knowledge, skills that you have learned, and innumerable small ideas — your own or of others. Dots also include successful as well as failed experiments carried out in the past by you or others. I hope it is clear now. When people talk about stealing ideas, they are basically referring to dots. And when they talk about original ideas, they refer to a completely new idea created by connecting the existing dots.

Every creative idea, every innovation, and every new invention is built on dots that already exist. Take the case of the celebrated inventor, Thomas Alva Edison. All his inventions were built on his own successful and failed experiments in the past that he carefully documented, apart from the experiments of other inventors.

The wow lies in the connections

All connect the dots, all the time. But why is the wow missing? The reason is that everyone connects the same, obvious dots. <u>If you connect the same dots in the same way you had been connecting, you will get the same, run-of-the-mill ideas that you had been getting.</u>

Connecting dots in a predictable manner won't result in a wow idea. And that's where creative people stand out. They connect dots differently.

The originality of the idea lies in its ***connections***.

"Originality often consists in linking up ideas whose connection was not previously suspected," wrote W.I.B. Beveridge[2] in *The Art of Scientific Investigation*. He further added, *"The role of the imagination is to create new meanings and to discover connections that, even if obvious, seem to escape detection."*

Surely, the way creative geniuses and innovative leaders connect the dots is different from the rest.

In the famous book[3] titled *The Innovator's DNA*, Jeff Dyer, Hal Gregersen, and Clayton M Christensen speak about an 8-year collaborative study to collect 360-degree data from over 500 innovators and over

5,000 executives in more than 75 countries to find out the origin of innovative and often, disruptive business ideas. The essence of their research was published in the bestselling book.

The authors of this book have identified five key skills associated with innovative and creative entrepreneurs. One of them is **association**. According to the authors, *"Creative minds connect the dots to make unexpected connections. They combine pieces of what may seem disparate pieces of information to get innovative new ideas."*

If you have been reading regularly on the subject of creativity, you might have come across various terms like "association", "cross-pollination", "cross-fertilization", "bisociation", "fusion", or even "sex" between the ideas. All mean the same things. In this book, I will be using the phrase "connecting the dots". After the next few chapters, you will understand the entire framework of creativity. The term "connecting the dots" is absolutely essential to help you understand the same.

If I have to summarize creativity in one line, I would say, *"Creativity is all about connecting the dots and creating a wow by connecting them in a way no one ever did."*

Going by the above, this is the section where "wow" begins!

Exercise

This exercise is designed to give you first-hand experience with connecting the dots.

Identify two different objects from your home that are completely unrelated. Your challenge is to combine them and create something novel and useful.

It need not be a breakthrough innovation. But at the same time, it should have some novelty and utility.

If it is possible to rip apart your household things and physically combine them, nothing like it. Please go ahead and do it. However, if it is not practical, then, for the time being, use your imagination to think of the combined product and draw it on paper or simply write down its description.

References

1. https://www.amazon.com/Steal-Like-Artist-Things-Creative-ebook/dp/B0074QGGK6/ref=sr_1_1?crid=3VDEDRMZPBT97&dchild=1&keywords=still+like+an+artist&qid=1622562271&s=digital-text&sprefix=still+like+an+ar%2Caps%2C806&sr=1-1
2. https://www.amazon.com/Art-Scientific-Investigation-W-I-B-Beveridge-ebook/dp/B075XDTKYW/ref=tmm_kin_swatch_0?_encoding=UTF8&qid=1622562180&sr=8-1
3. https://www.amazon.com/Innovators-DNA-Updated-New-Introduction-ebook/dp/B07FW898C1/ref=tmm_kin_swatch_0?_encoding=UTF8&qid=&sr=

Chapter 7 — *Always Be Connecting Diverse Dots*

Sir Richard Branson has a mantra for all his employees. The mantra is A-B-C-D. (Always Be Connecting Dots).

But before you jump to connecting dots, you need something…dots. If the dots are limited, so will the connections be. But even with a marginal increase in dots, your opportunity to connect them using different permutations and combinations increases exponentially. I have already said that the wow lies in connections. Creative geniuses are master connectors of dots. But before that, they are master **collectors** of dots. And this is what presents creative geniuses with infinitely greater opportunities to make unique connections when compared to others.

Hence, your pursuit of creativity should begin with a different A-B-C-D (Always Be **Collecting** Dots)

Always be *collecting* dots

"I have not failed. I've just found 10,000 ways that won't work."
— Thomas A. Edison

You must have already read or heard the above quote of Edison. People associate it with perseverance or a never-say-die spirit. But there is something more to it. Firstly, compared to the majority of people, Edison had a different way of looking at failure. In his scientific mind, failure didn't exist. For him, every failed experience was just feedback. Second, when he said, "…I've just found 10,000 ways that won't work," Edison was merely referring to the fact that he had already become rich by 10,000 dots. He knew the value of every dot. No wonder Edison was one of the greatest collectors of dots.

Collect lots of diverse dots

In the history of humanity, if there was one person who was a master of collecting diverse dots, he was Leonardo da Vinci. His diverse areas of interest included invention, painting, sculpting, architecture, science, music, mathematics, engineering, literature, anatomy, geology, botany, writing, history, and cartography.

When should you begin collecting dots?

The best time to start collecting dots was 10 years ago. The second best time to do so is now. Collecting the dots is always a continuous, ongoing process. You may never know, they could be handy to you any time, the way it happened with Steve Jobs.

Collect now, connect them when the opportunity comes

After dropping out of college, Steve Jobs decided to take a calligraphy class and learned a lot about calligraphy. Little did he know that he had added an important dot that would get connected in the future. In [the 2005 Stanford Commencement Address](), Steve Jobs recalls[1], *"None of this had even a hope of any practical application in my life. But ten years later, when we were designing the first Macintosh computer, it all came back to me. And we designed it all into the Mac. It was the first computer with beautiful typography."* He then goes on to make an important point, *"...of course, it was impossible to connect the dots looking forward when I was in college...you have to trust that the dots will somehow connect in your future..."*

How Edison built his dots bank

Earlier, we saw how Edison collected dots by dispassionately recording the outcomes of every single experiment rather than viewing it as a success or failure. Over the years, he built a 'dots bank' of innumerable experiments along with its outcomes. In the process, he built something else — an ability to see a pattern in the outcome of experiments carried out in one category and connect it with the other.

When Edison was confronted with the challenge of improving the quality of transmitted voice over the phone, he knew where to look for — his 'dots bank'. His trained mind connected the present challenge with an earlier failed project of transmitting Morse code. The outcome was the carbon transmitter that greatly improved the quality of transmitted voice.

Now it's time to connect the dots.

Always be connecting *diverse* dots

Let's revisit the mantra of Sir Richard Branson, A-B-C-D. (Always Be Connecting Dots).

Everyone can spot obvious connections and, therefore, come up with similar ideas. Creative people train themselves to make the most unlikely connections.

We, therefore, need a modified mantra, "Always Be Connecting **Diverse** Dots".

More the diversity, greater the wow

Maria Popova, in her popular blog, brainpicking, uses the analogy of LEGO building blocks to describe dots[2]. She states, "The more of these building blocks we have, and the more diverse their shapes and colors, the more interesting our castles will become."

Earlier, I referred to the famous book called *Innovator's DNA*. I want to bring your focus to two important terms that the authors used to describe the way creative people connect dots: The first one was *'unexpected connections'* and the other one being *"combining disparate pieces of information."*

How can you collect different types of dots?

You must have read somewhere that to become more creative, people recommend you make a conscious shift from your daily routine. This includes watching a different movie, watching a different TV serial, reading a book related to a completely different genre, talking a different route, etc.

This is because, following the same routine, you are getting exposed to the same set of dots. The different experiences will help you to create a different set of dots.

Besides, it will also make your brain more flexible, and therefore rewiring it will be much easier.

Connecting the unconnected

Earlier, I made mention of Vinci's diversity of interest. His wide areas of interest offered him the scope to make such disparate connections. But that's just half the story. What made him a genius is his ability to connect completely unrelated dots.

Michael J. Gelb extensively studied the life of Leonardo da Vinci and published a book[3]: _How to Think Like Leonardo da Vinci: Seven Steps to Genius Every Day._ One of the powerful lessons learned from Leonardo da Vinci is "Connect the unconnected."

In the words of Peter Fisk, the author of _Creative Genius: An Innovative Guide for Business Leaders, Border Crossers and Game Changers,_[4] "Leonardo was a master of cross-over. He combined ideas from animal and plant studies with psychology and fashion, anatomy, and architecture. From this, he formed his understanding of mechanics, and everything from hydraulic pumps to new musical instruments emerged. He used analogies; for example, he wrote short fables like Aesop, stories that seemed to be to entertain children but were, in fact, to communicate to adults the danger of greed and so on."

Connecting the diverse dots, the Steve Jobs way

It is rare to find someone who had mastered many fields as Da Vinci did. The good news is that you don't have to do that to make connections between dots from diverse fields. Those who connect such diverse dots are the ones who are always willing to learn new things. And when a challenge or an opportunity comes their way, they are always ready to make them part of a completely new connection.

Another such dot that Jobs collected was from a completely diverse area of Zen Buddhism.

This turned out to be a critical dot that influenced many business decisions that Jobs took when he chose NOT to have certain features in his products like a floppy drive in iMac, physical keyboard, and styles in iPhone.

The 'Zen connection' of Steve jobs and its impact on the business decisions of Apple is nicely brought to light by Jeff Yang in this article in

Wall Street Journal. He speaks about the concept of Ma which loosely translates as 'void' or 'gap' or 'space'. As explained by Jeff Yang *"Ma states that a thing is defined not just by what it is, but what it is not — that a sculpture is beautiful because of both the rock taken away and the rock left behind, and a ring is useful because of both the hollow at its center and the metal strip that surrounds it."*

The influence of *Ma* was not just limited to eliminating certain product features but also choosing NOT to launch countless products in the market. Given below is an excerpt from his interview with Betsy Morris published in Fortune magazine[5]. You can read the full interview here.

"Apple is a $30 billion company, yet we've got less than 30 major products. I don't know if that's ever been done before. Certainly, the great consumer electronics companies of the past had thousands of products. We tend to focus much more. People think focus means saying yes to the thing you've got to focus on. But that's not what it means at all. It means saying no to the hundred other good ideas that there are. You have to pick carefully. I'm actually as proud of many of the things we haven't done as the things we have done."

Intuition was another diverse dot that Jobs collected in a trip to India that he undertook before his Apple career began. In India, he realized that people have a far more developed intuition than the rest of the world and rely more on it than the intellect. Walter Isaacson, in his biography, quotes Steve Jobs: *"Intuition is a very powerful thing, more powerful than intellect, in my opinion. That's had a big impact on my work."*

Look for the dots at most unexpected places

Would you expect Nike's famous slogan 'Just do it' to have any connection with a murderer? I can almost see you shaking your head, saying, "No." Well, you are wrong. This is what 'making unexpected connections' is all about. Curious? Read on.

In an interview[6] with [Dezeen magazine](), Dan Wieden, the executive behind the famous slogan of Nike, offered a first-hand account of the genesis of "Just do it." He recalls his struggle to crack a creative tagline to form a common thread to connect seemingly unrelated TV commercials ready to be aired. That's when the name of Gary Gilmore popped up in his mind. Gary Gilmore was a murderer who was to be executed by a firing squad.

In the words of Dan Wieden, *"They asked him if he had any final thoughts, and he said: 'Let's do it'. I didn't like 'Let's do it', so I just changed it to 'Just do it'.*

So, different, unrelated TV commercials were like different dots that were not connecting. Finally, Wieden found a completely unrelated dot in the form of the last words of a murderer.

Suddenly, dots got connected, and the famous punchline was born.

Exercise

Today's exercise will give you a flavor of *collecting* the dots.

Think about all the different activities that you did during the last twenty-four hours. It could involve…

- Your interactions with different people
- Things you watched on TV
- Things you surfed on the internet like news, social media
- Mails or messages that you have received
- Books that you read

From all the above, you need to identify the ten things that struck you the most. You need to capture each of these things by using just one word.

For example, in the last twenty-four hours, you watched an adventure serial. One thing that struck you the most was the courage of the central character. Hence "courage" will be one of your dots.

Keep your list restricted only for the last twenty-four hours, don't include anything that has happened beyond it.

In the end, you have successfully *collected* ten dots.

References

1. https://news.stanford.edu/2005/06/14/jobs-061505/
2. https://www.brainpickings.org/2011/08/01/networked-knowledge-combinatorial-creativity/
3. https://www.amazon.com/How-Think-Like-Leonardo-Vinci-ebook/dp/B000SEFNF0/ref=tmm_kin_swatch_0?_encoding=UTF8&qid=&sr=
4. https://www.amazon.com/Creative-Genius-Innovation-Business-Crossers-ebook/dp/B0051H66W8
5. https://www.wsj.com/articles/BL-SEB-67363
6. https://archive.fortune.com/galleries/2008/fortune/0803/gallery.jobsqna.fortune/index.html
7. https://www.dezeen.com/2015/03/14/nike-just-do-it-slogan-last-words-murderer-gary-gilmore-dan-wieden-kennedy/

Chapter 8 — *Discover This Secret Treasure Of Diverse Dots*

Do you love watching or playing soccer or do you prefer indoor games like table tennis? Of course, both games are quite different. But they have one thing in common; they revolve around a round object called a ball. The same is true for many more games like cricket, hockey, volleyball, etc. In many ways, these balls resemble dots. I will come back to this in a short while.

Take this one minute challenge…now

I want you to attempt a quick exercise. I request you to open a separate word document or Evernote or simply grab an old-fashioned writing pad and a pen. I want you to make a list of as many round objects as you can think of in sixty seconds. Stop reading, set a timer, and start now. I won't mind waiting for a minute.

Frames: A little known secret of creativity

How many round objects could you jot down? Seven or seventeen? How many types of balls does your list comprise of? If the majority of the list are just different types of balls, then it means that the initial lines of this chapter have tricked you into thinking mainly about balls. I did this for a reason. And the reason was to make you understand the concept of frame.

<u>In learning creativity, the frame is the most important concept you need to understand and master to create countless dots (ideas).</u> Let me explain.

All the different types of balls that you jotted down fall under only one frame — balls.

In a similar manner, can you think of more frames comprising of round objects? Let's take wheels. Under this frame, you can prepare a long list of different kinds of wheels. Let me give you one more example — coins. Under the frame of coins, you can list down coins of different denominations. Want to load this frame even further? How about coins used in different countries? Go ahead and multiply coins of different denominations with the total number of countries in the world (196 —I just Googled to find out). This is not all. Add to the list different types of coins used in every country in the past 500 years. There is still more; multiply them with different metals like gold, silver, copper, etc. Suddenly, this frame called coins is overflowing with the treasure of wealth, or shall I say, the treasure of dots? Will there be many more frames of round objects? I can assure you, if you spend a few more seconds, you will be able to identify plenty of them. Each frame will be diverse from others. At the same time, inside each frame, there will be different types of dots (things).

I just gave examples of only three frames for round-shaped objects. I didn't dive deep into every frame. But I am sure you can imagine that these three frames alone could easily generate tons of dots.

How many dots do you think you would be able to generate by first thinking of more frames and thereafter finding dots inside each of them?

At the beginning of this book, I introduced to you the concept of dots. Just now, I brought up a new dimension of frames. Once you know the relationship between dots and frames, it won't be difficult for you to understand the secret that gives creative and innovative people the ability to generate infinite ideas. The world's most creative and innovative minds know that every new frame they identify will open a treasure trove of dots for them. Hence, they have built an ability to perform "multi-frame" thinking.

Earlier, I explained that you first need to create lots of dots and different types of dots to make a wow connection. For which you need the ability to generate lots of new ideas. In reality, this is an area most people struggle with. So, if you too find yourself struggling to generate lots of creative ideas, now you know what to do. **Stop thinking of dots, start focusing on frames**.

Henceforth, when confronted with any creative challenge, make it a habit **first to list only frames**. Once you are convinced that you have thought of a wide range of frames, start listing down ideas under each frame. At the end of the end, you will be flooded with not just countless dots (ideas), but diverse types of dots (ideas under different types of frames)

The implications of this concept of frames are profound. Have you fully realized that it's truly a game-changer? Let me summarize it to help you understand its implications.

Why do I call the concept of frames the profound one?

Because this concept can have an exponential impact on the quantity, diversity, and wow of your ideas.

1. **Quantity**—Frames are idea multipliers
2. **Diversity**—Every new frame opens the door to a diverse set of ideas
3. **Wow**—Multiple frames make it possible to connect completely different ideas (dots) and bring the wow

You have heard about out-of-the-box thinking. People loosely use it as a synonym for creativity. Did you realize? **Out-of-the-box thinking** is nothing but **out-of-the-frame thinking**, meaning connecting completely *unrelated* dots from two (or more) *different* frames.

Just now you learned the most powerful secret of creative thinking called "frames." If you want to discover new sets of dots (things or ideas), you need to discover new frames first. This is the secret all the creative minds of the world use to produce tons of ideas and effortlessly make connections between the completely diverse ones. With frames, now you have the power to multiply your ideas exponentially.

Once you learn to adapt to this new "multi-frame" way of thinking, the treasure trove of a large variety of dots awaits you. People struggle for a whole lifetime, trying to break their habit of thinking of the same set of dots inside a single frame. Luckily, you don't have to.

In a later part of this book, I will share a few powerful techniques to help you generate more frames. Once you practice and master them, multi-frame thinking and generating "ideas (dots) on demand" will become child's play.

Exercises

1

In the example of round objects, I mentioned three frames. Now have two challenges:

1. How many more frames can you create? Can you add seven more frames around round objects? It's possible. Don't give up so easily.
2. Fill every new frame with loads of dots. The total number of dots will be in hundreds, or maybe you will cross one thousand? Let's see.

Arrive at the number that should surprise you. The number should be such that **you should**

start believing yourself as an idea machine ⏹.

2

At this stage of the book, won't you like to check your progress? Have you acquired the ability to think of multiple options (frames)? Let's revisit brick's exercise for the third time. This time you approach it by applying your learning of frames.

First, take out the piece of a document where you attempted the brick exercise. Now, put all your answers under the broad frames. How many frames did you arrive at, two or three?

Now consciously try to think of completely different frames of using the bricks.

Could you create a greater number of frames?

3

Now it's time to *connect* the dots

Imagine you are a business consultant. Your client is struggling to achieve his growth objective. You have to give him ten tips that, when applied, will change the growth trajectory of his business.

Your today's challenge is to connect the dots.

Which are the dots that you need to connect?

One dot is constant, which is your client's business that is finding it difficult to grow. The other dots are the ones that you collected after completing the previous chapter! You have to connect those ten words, one by one, with the client's business in such a way that every connection results in some meaningful tip for your client.

Let me explain to you with one example.

During the exercise at the end of the previous chapter, "courage" was one dot that you collected. Now you need to connect it with the client's situation. Hence, one piece of advice to the client would be to think of some bold and unconventional approach, which is different from his competitors.

Similarly, try to connect the remaining dots with the client's business.

Section # 4 - Unleash your creative genius

Chapter 9 — *Break The Invisible Wall Around Creativity*

A cab driver didn't stop at the railway crossing, then jumped the signal. A nearby traffic officer, who was on duty, observed him doing so yet didn't stop him to issue the cab driver a ticket for violating the law. Why?

A man who lives in a thirty-six-story building jumps out of his window. Incredibly, he survives without any injury. How is this possible?

Could you solve the above puzzles instantly? If you are still struggling to find the answers, it is because certain **assumptions** are blocking you from seeing the obvious answer.

(In section 2, we discussed five creativity blocks. Your set of hidden assumptions is the sixth one, which is most critical. I wanted to introduce it at the appropriate stage of your journey of creativity, which happens to be this section.)

(You can see the answers to the above puzzle at the end of the book. Meanwhile, please read on.)

Our assumptions are like imaginary walls around our minds that we believe to be real. As a result, our mind is unable to think of different or out-of-the-box ideas that lie beyond these walls.

<u>Creative ideas and innovation just can't come into existence as long as assumptions exist.</u>

Edison knew this quite well. As the story goes, before hiring anyone for the post of research assistant, Edison would invite the interviewee to a local café and order him a bowl of soup. Any candidate who added salt to the soup without tasting it would be immediately rejected. Edison always believed that any individual with many built-in assumptions is a complete misfit for a position that demands creativity as a mandatory skill.

Assumptions come in a disguise of facts and blind us to the obvious

A large majority of things that we consider as facts are just assumptions. They blind our vision, making it impossible for us to see the obvious. Take the case of Swiss watchmakers. Once, they ruled the global watchmaking industry. At some point, they made around 65% of all the watches in the world. This success created enormous wealth for the Swiss watchmakers. It also created a set of 'facts' based on which the entire Swiss watch industry operated successfully for a long period. Now, what were those facts?

Fact # 1: A watch has to be mechanical.

Fact # 2: It needs to have wheels, levers, gears, and mainsprings.

Fact # 3: It needs to tick.

Interestingly, Max Hetzel, who was a scientist working for a Swiss watchmaking company, challenged all these assumptions and invented a quartz watch that was even more accurate than the mechanical ones. Overnight, all the 'facts' mentioned above became just a bunch of assumptions. The story didn't end here. He took his invention to many Swiss watchmaking companies, who outright rejected it. For them, the points stated above were still facts. And a watch that didn't comply with the facts couldn't be a real one. Hetzel then showcased his invention at the World Watch Congress. The Americans and the Japanese just took one look at it, and the rest is history.

Assumptions blinded the Swiss watchmakers from seeing an obvious opportunity and resulted in their downfall. The American and Japanese watchmakers didn't have the baggage of assumptions and, therefore, could clearly see a big opportunity in the novel invention of a quartz watch.

How deep-rooted are your assumptions?

Do you think you would have behaved differently if you were in the shoes of the Swiss watchmakers? Do you think you can spot your hidden assumptions? Try solving this puzzle.

The Dilemma

You are driving down the road in your car on a wild, stormy night. You pass by a bus stop and see three people waiting for the bus:
1. An old lady who looks as if she is about to die.
2. An old friend who once saved your life.

3. The perfect partner you have been dreaming about.

Knowing that there can only be one passenger in your car, whom would you choose?

Did you figure the answer out? Let me give you a hint. Your assumption is stopping you from getting the answer. Remove it, and you will see that the answer to this puzzle is pretty obvious.

Was the hint useful? Could you finally solve it? If you are still struggling, then here is the answer: The old lady, of course! After helping the old lady into the car, you can give your keys to your friend and wait with your perfect partner for the bus.

In hindsight, doesn't it seem to be the most obvious answer? The reason you couldn't get it was mainly due to two assumptions **1.** YOU have to be necessarily driving the car and, therefore, can choose only one person inside the car. **2.** The ones who will be left at the bus stop were destined to experience a horrible night. Most interestingly, despite hinting to you that your *assumption* is stopping you from seeing the obvious, you were unable to identify it and challenge it.

Now you know how difficult it is to spot our deep-rooted assumptions. This is where creative and innovative minds score over the rest.

Mind you, no one deliberately forms the assumptions. They get formed below the level of consciousness. We can call them "unconscious assumptions", but for the concerned person, those are the "realities."

Challenge every reality

The only way one can separate assumptions from reality is by challenging them. But we believe our assumptions to be the reality. Hence, to challenge them, you must question all the things that are believed to be real. When you look at history, you will realize that almost all the innovations and inventions happened only when someone successfully challenged and proved that certain things that were believed as realities were just assumptions. In your journey towards mastering creativity, challenging such deeply ingrained realities is one of the toughest yet most important milestones that you must cross.

How challenging the "realities" changed the fortune of General Motors (GM)

In the year 1923, when Alfred Sloan took over as the CEO of General Motors (GM), the market was dominated by Ford Motor. Ford's famous Model T was ruling the roost. That was the era when Henry Ford had famously quoted, *"You can have any color you want, as long as it is black."*

Behind the above statement of Ford, there were few "realities."

Reality # 1—The price of the car was not within reach for many.

Reality # 2—To attract more customers, one needs to bring down its price as much as possible.

Reality # 3—Improving efficiency through mass production was the way to bring down the manufacturing cost and the price to the consumer.

Reality # 4—The only way a customer could buy a new car was by paying cash or taking a loan.

Reality # 5—Painting a car with any color involved a cumbersome process that took several days to dry. Compared to all the other color paints, black enamel paint was the only option that took fewer days to dry.

In the given market scenario, to break Ford's stranglehold over the market, the only option left to Sloan was to challenge all these realities and come up with some innovative solution.

Sloan did exactly the same. He did it so successfully that in less than five years, Ford Motor Company stopped the production of the Model T!

What exactly did Sloan do? How could he break these "realities"? It's another fascinating story. I strongly recommend you read this interesting piece written in LinkedIn[1]—What Organizations Can Learn from Alfred Sloan, Not Henry Ford, by Rachna Choudhry.

Here is a powerful technique that can help you liberate your creativity from the shackles of assumptions.

Reversing the assumptions

This technique consists of the following steps:

State your assumptions. (Since initially you would see all your assumptions as facts, list down all the facts pertaining to your situation.)

Ask yourself: What is its opposite?

Replace a few words in the statement with a new set of words that turn the meaning of the sentence into an opposite one.

The reversed idea will be opposite to what you, as well as everyone, had been believing all these years. It may sound completely outrageous to you. Your first impulse may be to drop it altogether. But don't do it. Follow the next step.

Ask yourself: Why might it be true?

Start searching for reasons that will support the reversed statement. Do it for every reversed idea. Don't think of the feasibility of any of the reversed ideas at this stage. We are going to address that bit in the next step. As you keep trying harder, answers will start appearing. Each answer will offer you a new frame, and every frame will be loaded with the dots of exciting possibilities. This is the stage when *Aha! moments* happen. Earlier, you had one reality that was confining you. Now you have many new realities that might actually liberate you. If you could apply this technique successfully, you have an innovative solution in hand.

Ask yourself: How can I make these ideas happen?

This is the stage where you will figure out ways to make your crazy ideas happen. List down every possible way you could think of to execute all the ideas. Remember, in the beginning, you can never find an end-to-end and one hundred percent doable solution. In fact, some of the solutions may appear either half-baked or too far-fetched. But don't discard any of it. More dots will get connected later. For the time being, keep creating more dots. Do it individually. Do it along with your core group. It might take you a few days or even weeks to complete this exercise.

Successfully reversing assumptions transformed an Indian city

To understand how reversing assumptions can bring dramatic results, let us go through the case study of one city of India:

Trichy is a city located in the southern part of India. Around 1999, the city had witnessed terrorist activities. Communal tension was at its peak. Crime rates were high. The threat of further terrorist attacks was looming large.

Compared to global standards, the police force was operating at one-third the size. Not only was the police force small, but the people regarded it as their enemy too.

To make matters worse, the police information and intelligence system were at their weakest.

Both the police and politicians agreed unanimously that they needed more cops, more intelligence, more equipment, and tougher measures to improve the situation.

India's Prime Minister's visit to the city was just a month away. However, the fear of possible terrorist attacks was giving the concerned officials sleepless nights.

At this stage, a new man, J. K. Tripathy, took over as the Commissioner of Police in Trichy. Tripathy had a seemingly insurmountable task cut out for him.

Now, let us apply the technique of reversing assumptions to the above situation:

Assumptions

1: People regard police constables as their *enemies*.

2: More sophisticated types of equipment *are needed* to improve intelligence.

3: *More* cops are needed to control the situation.

What is its opposite?

1: People regard police constables as their *friends*.

2: More sophisticated types of equipment are *not needed* to improve intelligence.

3: *Fewer* cops are needed to control the situation.

Why might it be true?

1: Perception of the police force is just a reflection of the behavior they demonstrate. Therefore, it is possible that by adopting a completely new people-friendly behavior, the police department could be perceived as friends.

2: Intelligence lies with people, not with equipment. Due to a lack of trust in the police, people were withholding information. Once the perception changes, the police department wouldn't have any problem receiving a steady flow of intelligence.

3: It's quality, not quantity, that matters. A small group of honest, dedicated cops will deliver results that are a hundred times better than a large group of corrupt and indifferent police personnel. At present, the police department struggles to control the situation due to a lack of trust and intelligence. Hence, it appears like there's a need for more cops. But once the people change their perception of the police, become supportive, and start sharing intelligence, even a smaller police force will become effective.

How can I make these ideas happen?

By ensuring that the police personnel change their behavior towards the people and win their trust. Once it is achieved, make a select set of people partners in the process. They will play the role of the eyes and ears of the police department.

This is what Tripathy did. He took a series of measures listed below that brought about a transformational change.

Tripathy's immediate action was to ensure that the police made a shift in their mindset — instead of seeing themselves as enforcers who are distinct from the community to being part of the community. This new mindset brought about a new set of actions. As a result, people started seeing the cops as their friends and protectors.

Simultaneously, Tripathy experimented with a select group of 50 police constables with impeccable track records and asked them to operate from their homes for one week. Their job was to blend in with the people, listen and observe what was happening, and share it with him regularly. This resulted in a big jump in the amount of information that started flowing into the department.

Having tasted big success with this experiment, Tripathy decided to scale it up. Out of the total strength of 2,600 police personnel, Tripathy handpicked 260 of the most honest ones. He divided the city into 60 localities called 'beats'. Each of the beats was assigned to four constables from the group of 260 handpicked cops. These 'beat officers', as they were called, were empowered with a great degree of freedom. As a result, each of the beats was operated with total ownership. These 260 beats worked assiduously in bringing about police-public partnership, thereby ensuring improved perception in the minds of the general public, improved flow of information, and finally, reduction in crime rates.

Tripathy made himself available to anyone who wanted to share any information or suggestions.

He circulated his mobile number through local press, TV, radio, etc. In addition, he would meet around 50 people every day in his office.

The result that this Trichy experiment brought was nothing short of dramatic. Crime rates dropped to one-fifth of the original numbers. Crime detection increased from 74% to 95%. Recovery of stolen properties rose from 41% to 91%. But most importantly, Trichy, a city that was a hotbed of communal disturbance, was transformed into a peaceful city.

The above details offer you just a glimpse. The entire story is even more fascinating. You can read it in the book[2], written by Porus Munshi, *Making Breakthrough Innovation Happen*. As the book's title suggests, it is packed with 11 such fascinating stories, and each of them is about breakthrough innovation. It's a must-read book for anyone interested in the subject of innovation.

Below is a list of a few of the assumptions that stop people from asking questions (Mind you, these are just a few. The actual list might go up to hundreds):

- I know this subject like the back of my hand. There is nothing more that I need to learn.
- I know where he/she is heading to, we have tried it before, and it won't work.
- Asking questions speaks of a lack of knowledge.
- It's the same old story. I have heard it several times before.

- Asking too many questions will make me appear confused.
- I am well aware of such situations. I already know the answer.
- As a leader, my job is to offer answers, not questions.
- My boss expects me to come up with answers, not questions.
- I want to be perceived as an expert. Asking basic questions will make me seem like a novice.

This brings us to an interesting contradiction:

What do you need to challenge assumptions? Questions.
What is stopping you from asking questions? Assumptions.

Fortunately, I have given you a powerful technique to challenge your assumptions. Apply it to all the assumptions that are stopping you from asking questions. This will be of great help as you move to the next chapter, which is all about asking questions to ignite your creativity.

Exercise

In this exercise, you will practice applying the reversal technique. The best place to do it is on your own challenges.

Let's revisit the document consisting of your goals and challenges. In that document, you have already listed down your challenges.

The first step is to write down all the present realities pertaining to your challenge. This you will do to all your challenges. Then follow all the steps of the reversal technique as described in this chapter. Can you think of any ways to make the opposite statement work? Try hard. Think deep. Because you are likely to get some breakthrough ideas here.

Please make a note of all the new ideas that come to your mind. You may think some of them are still half-baked or not feasible. Still, note them down. You will find them useful during future exercises.

References

1. https://www.linkedin.com/pulse/what-organizations-can-learn-from-alfred-sloan-henry-ford-choudhry/

2. https://www.amazon.com/Making-Breakthrough-Innovation-Happen-TheImpossible/dp/817223774X/ref=sr_1_1?dchild=1&keywords=Making+Breakthrough+Innovation+Happen&qid=1622798904&s=books&sr=1-1

Chapter 10 — *Change Your Question, Challenge Your Realities*

"I am stuck! I can't think of any better idea," is the common expression that we hear. Here, by "stuck", what the person is referring to are the ideas (that are stuck).

Have you wondered where exactly the ideas get stuck?

Ideas get stuck at two places: **1.** Inside the invisible walls of assumptions **2.** Inside a single frame.

Let's ask ourselves a couple of questions:

Question: Why do ideas get stuck?

Answer: Questions

When you ask the same set of questions, you get the same set of ideas. And you are stuck.

Question: What is the way to get unstuck?

Answer: Questions

When you change your questions, you break the invisible wall of assumptions and find a new set of frames. And you are unstuck.

Questions are the key to liberating your creativity.

It shouldn't come to you as a surprise. In the initial part of this book, I shared the research that showed how as children grow up, the number of questions they ask comes down drastically, and a clear correlation between the age-related decrease in the number of questions and dwindling creativity.

In the last two chapters, we have covered a couple of profound secrets:

1. How identifying and busting **assumptions** can unshackle your creativity.
2. How **multi-frame thinking** can help you exponentially increase your ideas.

Changing your questions is a single key to accomplish both the above things.

How do questions break the invisible wall of assumptions?

I have already answered this question in the chapter on assumptions. Remember Reversal Technique? The whole technique is based on answering a set of carefully chosen questions, asked in a proper sequence.

Reframe your challenge

In his famous book, *Seven Habits of Highly Effective People*, Stephen Covey shares an example of a person climbing efficiently on a ladder, only to discover that the ladder has been leaning against the wrong wall.

This holds good even with the problem that we are trying to tackle. Changing our questions will help us discover the right wall, meaning the right way of defining our challenge. This process is known as **reframing.**

How to reframe your challenge

When you look at the same situation from a higher level, it gives you a different perspective. This also applies to the challenge that you are attempting to crack. The process of reframing involves asking a series of searching questions to probe your intent or objective deeply. This will help you to see our problem from a new or higher perspective. Then, based on this new perspective, you reframe your challenge.

Let me explain this with an example. Imagine yourself as a start-up needing more funds to meet your present and future requirements. You are looking for a Venture Capitalist (VC) to fund your business, and you are perhaps working hard to come up with different ideas to convince VCs to fund your business. If you list down all the possible ideas that you can think of, they will be relatively small in number. If, for whatever reason, it is not working for you, you have no other option. You are stuck. The reason you are stuck is because of your assumption that to raise the finance, you need VC funding. As long as you continue to operate with this assumption, your options will remain limited.

How about stepping back and asking yourself a few questions.

What is that I am looking for?

I am looking for more ideas to convince venture capitalists to fund my business.

Why do you have to convince the venture capitalists?

Because I need more funds to run my business.

So, what does your business need?

It needs more finance.

Okay, so if getting more money is your objective, how will you frame your challenge?

My question would be, "What are the possible options I can explore to raise finance for my business?"

The original question, *"How do I convince venture capitalists to fund my business?"* is now reframed.

Now, you start exploring many possibilities like crowdfunding, sponsorships, tie-ups, partnerships, loans, and many more options to raise funds. The hidden assumption of venture capitalists as the only source of finance gets busted. The invisible barrier is broken.

Puzzles and jokes

We struggle with many puzzles because our brain is wired to think in a single frame. The moment we shift our frame, the answers to impossible-sounding problems suddenly become obvious to us. During creativity workshops, many hard-boiled business leaders are put off whenever some puzzle-related group activity is introduced. They find it too kiddish and unconnected with their business reality. But in reality, regularly solving puzzles is a powerful way to rewire your brain and learn a new skill of finding different frames.

The same applies to jokes. What makes them so funny is that they lead you through a wrong frame and change the frame when you least expect it. Here is an example:

Early one morning, a mother went to her sleeping son and woke him up.

"Wake up, son. It's time to go to school."
"But why, Mum? I don't want to go to school."

"Give me two reasons why you don't want to go to school."
"One, all the children hate me. Two, all the teachers hate me..."

"Oh! That's no reason. Come on, you have to go to school!"
"Give me two good reasons WHY I should go to school?"

"One, you are FIFTY-TWO years old. Two, you are the HEADMASTER."

How changing the questions created breakthrough innovation

In 2007, Brian Chesky and Joe Gebbia were living in a spacious rented flat in San Francisco. As you know, the bigger the flat, the higher the rent. Their financial position was a little tight, and hence were struggling to pay their rent. The question they were asking—*How can we make more money to pay our rent comfortably?* A pretty common question, isn't it? As long as they kept asking themselves the same question, nothing happened. They were stuck. One fine day, they asked a different question — *Is there any way we could use the extra space of our flat to help us make extra money and pay the rent?*

This question replaced the old reality with a new one that brought them to a new possibility.

The old reality—Bigger the flat, higher the rent. Hence, greater the liability.

The new reality—Bigger the flat, greater the opportunity to make some extra money.

It's a natural law of the universe that once you start looking for opportunities, they start appearing.

The opportunity appeared in the form of an upcoming conference in San Francisco, which had a heavy demand for hotels. Since they had already changed their question, they could immediately spot it. So they hurriedly designed a website, bought a few mattresses, and hosted three guests during the conference, each paying the rent of $80.

They were thrilled to see their idea turning into easy cash. But if they were to stop at that, an innovative business idea called Airbnb would have never been born. Fortunately, they didn't. Brian Chesky, Joe Gebbia, and Nathan Blecharczyk, the three co-founders of Airbnb, started sensing a big opportunity in their idea. And came the next question: *How can we scale it up?*

The reality—They couldn't. Because to scale up this model, they would need a huge renting space and huge funds.

To challenge this reality, they needed to ask one more question. And they asked:

How can we scale it up without any additional investment?

The dots were there in two different frames that were invisible to everyone. The new questions broke invisible barriers and made them visible.

1. Countless people were happy to make extra income using their existing space.
2. An equal number of people were looking for affordable and homely places to spend their nights.

They found the answers they were looking for. The **extra space** would come from the flat owned by **others**. In other words, they needed more people like them, with extra space, who are willing to rent it out. They swung into action, enrolling thousands of people in their new business model. It required lots of hard work.

They had their share of disappointments and setbacks. But they didn't allow them to dampen their resolve. Once they had the dot in the form of extra space from the flat owned by others. They connected it with the other dot of people looking out for affordable and homely places to spend their nights.

Once the dots got connected, the disruptive business model came into existence.

I can't stress enough the benefits of asking questions for challenging assumptions. Once you learn to do it effortlessly, you can open practically any door of opportunity.

Treating the existing realities as assumptions and challenging them requires courage. That's what one advertising agency did and reaped the high reward, as agency people are among the most creative bunch of people. In this case, they changed their question, added their creativity, and took some bold action. The result? Please read on.

How asking different question helped the agency bag a lucrative account

British Rail had once invited creative ad agencies for a pitch. During such pitches, agencies are expected to propose their best creative ideas. The prospective client would sit through all the agency presentations and award the contract to the one that they find most creative among all. This is how things work. This is the well-accepted practice (reality) of the advertising industry.

Every agency asked themselves: *How can we present our creative work to the prospective client in order to stand out from the rest?* This question had an in-built assumption: To win an account, you need to make an effective presentation. But one agency asked a different type of question: *What kind of experience do we need to give the prospective client to stand out from the rest?* This slight tweaking of the question by changing one word — *presentation* to *experience* — opened up a new set of possibilities (frames).

The agency challenged one more common practice (assumption) of making the pitch in the prospective client's office. Instead, they requested the prospective client to come to their office. As the story goes, the top executives of British Rail were kept waiting in a dirty reception for more than half an hour. As their patience waned and they were about to leave, the agency executives stopped them and greeted them with the line, "That, gentlemen, is what confronts your customers every day. Let us now show you how you can rectify your image."

The whole experience was so profound that it provided an instant answer to the question that the executives of British Rail were asking: *Which is the most creative ad agency to award the contract to?*

Those who ask different questions to challenge the assumptions and dare to take bold action always enjoy a competitive advantage over the rest.

I hope, by now, you are clear on how questions help you remove the assumptions that block our creative thinking.

But this is only a small part. In the next chapter, you will learn how to use questions to unleash your creative genius by shifting to new frames.

Exercise

In the previous exercise, by applying the reversal technique, could you get any breakthrough ideas to crack the challenges coming in the way of your most important audacious goal?

In this exercise, you will try to reframe your challenge.

The process of reframing involves having a second look at your challenges by taking a step backward and asking a different set of questions.

Like the previous exercise, you will begin this exercise with a piece of document wherein you have written down all your challenges.

In this chapter, I have given examples of venture capitalist funding and that of the ad agency. Now you have to ask different questions by applying the learning from those examples to your challenges.

The answers to the questions might give a completely new perspective to your challenges.

References

1. https://www.amazon.in/Habits-Highly-Effective-People-Powerful-ebook/dp/B08KH29CJC/ref=tmm_kin_swatch_0?_encoding=UTF8&qid=1624693103&sr=1-1-spons

Chapter 11 — *Change Your Frame, Change Your Game*

How can questions help you to discover new frames?

Here, I would like to given the essence of what we discussed so far:

<u>Your questions determine the frame into which the answer falls. If you are unable to get new ideas and feel stuck, it means you are stuck in the single or limited frames. As long as you keep asking the same set of questions, the answers will take you to the same frame(s). The key is changing your questions. When you change your questions, the new set of answers will take you to a different set of frames.</u>

"Change your questions and change your frames."

Which are those questions that will help you discover new frames?

I wish I could give you a list of questions that would do a job for you. But things don't work that way. You have to keep trying different approaches.

Let me share with you different approaches with examples.

Shift the focus from "you" to "them"

Do you find it tough to solve problems that involve other people? Take a closer look at the questions that you are asking yourself. Perhaps, your questions revolve around your own wants. Change your focus. Put yourself in the other person's shoes. Try understanding his/her pain areas. Now ask questions looking at the same situation from the other's point of view. How does your new question look? When you try answering it, in all probability, it will lead you to a new set of frames.

Michael Michalko, in his book[1] _Cracking Creativity—The Secrets of Creative Genius,_ shares an anecdote from Toyota. The company was grappling with the problem of improving workers' productivity. Initially, the management asked employees for ideas on how they could become more productive. This question was confined to a frame, namely efficiency, which appeared to be serving management's interest. The employees were not interested. The management received very few responses. Then management decided to shift the focus to the employees' needs and asked a different question — *How can you make your job easier?* This question opened up many possibilities (frames). As the results show, the management was flooded with more suggestions than they could handle.

Replace a word

In the previous chapter, you saw how a slight tweak in the question helped the ad agency win a big and prestigious contract.

Let's take another example. Imagine that next month is your parent's fiftieth wedding anniversary. Instead of asking, "How do we celebrate their anniversary?", you can change your question to, "How can I give my parents a surprise to make the event the most memorable one?" The words "surprise" and "memorable" in the place of "celebrate" suddenly bring so many exciting possibilities.

Ask why

Inventors and scientists have an insatiable curiosity to know more about things. Their curious minds are not content by asking the same set of questions that everyone asks. Their curiosity drives them to ask different types of questions. When others see things and accept them as usual, day-to-day happening, scientists find them intriguing. When a fruit falls from a tree, there is nothing unusual about it. But when an apple fell on Newton's head, it triggered a series of questions that resulted in the discovery of the law of gravity.

Albert Einstein, one of the greatest geniuses who lived in this world, knew the importance of asking the right question. He once said, *"If I had an hour to solve a problem and my life depended on the solution, I would spend the first fifty-five minutes determining the proper question to ask, for once I know the proper question, I could solve the problem in less than five minutes."*

Ask why not

The history of medical science has many inventions that have impacted the health and survival of the human race. If you have to single out one of the biggest such inventions, the smallpox vaccine will surely be one of them. In the 20th century, smallpox was responsible for around 300 to 500 million deaths. About 30% of people infected with smallpox died. And those who survived had to live with scars or even blindness permanently.

For centuries, scientists were trying to battle this demon without any success. Everyone was asking questions like 'Why are people suffering from smallpox?' or 'How can we prevent people from getting infected?' Edward Jenner asked a completely different question. He wondered **why** milkmaids were **not** getting infected with smallpox. This question changed the frame and connected the dot called smallpox with a new one — cowpox. The focus shifted to a cowpox-causing virus that belongs to the same family as smallpox but as a much milder form. This new connection resulted in the invention of a vaccine for smallpox.

I have shared quite a few examples of game-changing inventions and innovations. The inventors, innovators, and creative geniuses are truly game-changers. They all know the secret of asking different questions to change their frames.

The **"game changers"** are the **"frame changers"**

Isn't this a "frame-changing" revelation for you?

If you have to take just one learning from this book, learn how to be a "frame changer."

Change your questions by wearing different hats

Here is another powerful way of thinking of different questions that you otherwise may not ask.

Put on the imaginary hats of those great minds who had mastered the art of asking insightful questions.

Think of the famous real or fictitious personalities and one attribute that you strongly associate with them. Now, keeping their dominant attribute in mind, ask yourself, for cracking your challenge, what question will they ask?

Let me explain with a few examples.

Imagine that I am looking for some breakthrough ideas to take my business to the next orbit.

I start with wearing an imaginary hat of Steve Jobs. In Chapter 4, I mentioned that when other mobile phone marketers were asking about features they needed to *add*, Steve Jobs asked about the features that he needed to *eliminate*. So, adapting the approach of Steve Jobs, the question that I ask will be, *"What should I stop doing to bring a sharp focus to my business?"* This will force me to critically look at everything that I am doing and perhaps discover something of lesser importance but take away a good amount of my time and resources. Hence, I need to stop it, to bring greater focus on those areas that matter the most.

Now I wear an imaginary hat of Jeff Bezos. The most striking thing I find about Jeff Bezos is his obsession with putting customer interest ahead of everything. So, my question will be, "Is there anything more I need to do to offer my customers the best value?" The answer to this might result in finding out a differentiating idea that will bring huge value to the customer and give my business a competitive advantage.

Finally, I wear an imaginary hat of Sherlock Holmes. When I think of Sherlock Holmes, a conversation from a book called *Silver Blaze* flashes my mind.

Inspector Lestrade: *"Is there any point to which you would wish to draw my attention?"*

Holmes: *"To the curious incident of the dog in the nighttime."*

Lestrade: *"The dog did nothing in the nighttime."*

Holmes: *"That was the curious incident."*

When everyone was searching for things that *happened* on the night of the theft, Sherlock Holmes diverted his trained mind towards the direction of what *did not happen*. That's where he spotted a valuable clue that no one could see.

In the above anecdote, I see a great value in analyzing a given situation in a different way — by **looking beyond the obvious**. I will apply this learning to my customers. Perhaps the question I had been asking earlier is, "What are customers saying about my product or service?". Instead, my new question will be, "What are my customers not saying about products or services that I offer?" This might bring up some insight that I might have completely overlooked.

You have seen how this exercise of wearing the imaginary hat of different personalities helped me to find a completely new set of questions. These new questions led me to the discovery of different frames. These were just a few examples. While working on a real challenge, you use this method with more personalities.

In the previous chapter, I mentioned reframing the challenge. Let me share my first-hand experience.

How changing the question helped me to reframe my problem

In a brainstorming session with my colleagues, we hit upon the idea of creating a new entity or a professional stream called 'patient educators' in the arena of Indian healthcare. This initiative involved starting and running an education institute. We had to create it literally out of thin air. I was leading this initiative with the help of a young, bright team of management trainees.

We had two major challenges. First to create a roadmap and then to execute it. Execution involved networking, tying up with experts from different streams of healthcare and roping them as visiting faculty, besides striking deals with government and non-government bodies to accredit our program.

The immediate challenge was to prepare a road map. But we were confronted with a big challenge — The project we had undertaken had no parallel in our industry. All we saw around us were clouds of ambiguity. We didn't have the slightest idea of where to start. We had no option but to find a way through the complexities and ambiguities. We used to have tons of brainstorming sessions and were slowly connecting different dots.

Around the same time, a new person joined our team. Let's call him Rajan. He was fresh from a B-school, bright, enthusiastic, and most importantly, quite passionate about the project. We badly needed someone to bring in a fresh perspective to our thought process.

But I was in for a big disappointment!

There was very little contribution from his end and practically no fresh ideas. Initially, I told myself, "he needs some time to get a grip on the project." So I decided to be patient with him and started spending extra time explaining the nuances of the project to him. But the outcome continued to remain the same.

Then I thought, "This boy looks promising. Perhaps he needs coaching." I tried coaching him, but that didn't help either.

Worst still, during several occasions, when he was asked to get back to me with his thoughts, he would avoid it on some pretext or the other.

I was losing my patience. I repeatedly started asking myself, "How can I nail Rajan down and make him contribute to the thought process?"

I tried many things, but nothing was working. Perhaps, we had made a wrong selection.

Then it struck me. I was stuck inside a single frame. I needed to discover a different frame. To do that, I needed to change my question.

I went back to the question that I had been asking myself — *"How can I make Rajan contribute to the thought process?"*

I took a step back and asked myself a few searching questions. My thought process went something like this:

If I have to look at the bigger picture, what am I trying to achieve?

I am trying to ensure the successful completion of the project.

In order to ensure the successful completion of the project, what do I expect from the team?

I expect every team member to contribute to the success of the project.

What do I expect from Rajan?

As I do with every other team member, I also expect Rajan to contribute towards the project's success.

Changing my question from *"How can I make Rajan contribute to the thought process?"* to "How *can I make Rajan contribute towards the project's success?"* opened a new set of possibilities. Rajan's strength lay in execution besides being great at networking. For our project, we had to get an audience with different stakeholders and work out arrangements with them. We were also looking for accreditations from universities and government bodies. I realized that Rajan was just the man needed for such tasks. When I discussed these revised expectations, I could see a new, confident Rajan eager to prove himself. The speed with which he struck deals with different stakeholders and also got accreditations surprised everyone. All this meant a lot for the success of the project.

It was a great learning moment for me. I had first-hand experience of the power of reframing.

Okay, now it's time to put your new learning into practice. The exercise at the end of this chapter is extremely important.

Exercise

I have shared many techniques to change your questions and discover new frames. The key lies in practice. As you keep practicing, asking such "frame-changing" questions will become your second nature. In the process, you will also discover some new ways of asking questions.

This exercise will help you understand a step-by-step approach to applying the techniques you have just learned.

1. **State your challenge**— After doing previous exercises, some of your challenges might have been modified. But this step remains constant. It is important to write down your challenges. It helps in crystallizing your thoughts. Besides, you may need to revisit them at a later stage.
2. **State your present questions**—Take a separate document and write down the present set of questions that you are asking for each of the challenges. This is your worksheet.
3. **Change your questions**—Start applying, one by one, all the techniques of changing your questions that I have shared in this chapter. In addition to this, ask a few more questions by using who, what, where, when, why, and how. Also, include the "what if" question in your list. Keep trying with every technique till you are satisfied that the

revised question has enough "frames juice" in it. Once you are done, write down all the new questions.
4. **Reframe your challenge**—Revisit your challenge statement. Do any of the questions reframe your challenge? Do you think the reframed challenge brings a different perspective and offers you more possibilities? If that is the case, write down the reframed challenge statement below the earlier one.
5. **Create new frames**—Revisit the document with all the questions written on it. Start asking a new set of questions one by one. Are the answers to these questions leading you to new frames? Think hard to search for a new frame for every question and write it down on a separate document. Once you finish asking all the questions, you would have found out many new frames. This means now you have created many alternatives to address your challenge.

References

1. https://www.amazon.com/Cracking-Creativity-Secrets-Creative-Genius/dp/1580083110/ref=sr_1_1?dchild=1&keywords=cracking+creativity&qid=1622895982&s=books&sr=1-1

Section # 5 - Your Subconscious Mind

Chapter 12 — *Where Do Wow Ideas Come From?*

Hieron, the king of Syracuse, suspected that the new gold crown was not pure gold as claimed by the goldsmith. Archimedes was tasked to figure out the exact truth. Archimedes knew the density of gold. So, theoretically, Archimedes knew that if he could calculate the volume of the crown, then the density of the crown could be calculated and compared with the density of the gold. If two densities were different, then it would be proven that the crown was adulterated. However, given the irregular shape of the crown, Archimedes could not think of any way to measure its volume without damaging the crown.

Archimedes thought long and hard but could not find a method for proving that the crown was not solid gold. He was stuck. He decided to take a break and go out for a bath. As he stepped into the bathtub, the water level rose, and it spilled out of the tub. He realized that the water displaced by his body was equal to the weight of his body. He instantly knew that he had found the solution to the problem.

He jumped out of the tub. Forgetting that he was without his clothes, he went out running

naked on the street shouting "Eureka!"
(Meaning "I have found it.")

Because of the above story of Archimedes, the moments of epiphany are often described as eureka moments. Some refer to it as *aha moments*. My favorite way of describing them is wow moments. In the subsequent chapters, I will use the above terms interchangeably.

Let's revisit the story of Archimedes. Archimedes, who was one of the sharpest minds in the fields of physics and mathematics, couldn't solve the problem while he was **thinking** hard over it. The problem got solved at the moment when he was **not thinking** about it. Doesn't it sound strange? From where did the solution appear?

The answer is the subconscious mind.

The above story is a classic example of how our subconscious mind presents us with such eureka moments, literally from nowhere.

Let me explain how the subconscious mind works with the help of an analogy.

Imagine a meeting is in progress. The boss is seeking ideas from his team. Among the group, there is one member who is quite vocal. He is quite knowledgeable about the subject, has an analytical mind, and has a lot to share. He brings so many angles on the subject. But somehow, dots are not getting connected. The wow ideas that the boss is looking for are missing.

There is another member who is quiet throughout, only listening to the others. The one who had been quite vocal receives a call from one of his important customers and excuses himself from the meeting. Once this vocal member is out, the quiet one starts speaking. As he speaks, he connects many unrelated dots. Suddenly, there are so many wow ideas!

The vocal participant from the above analogy is our conscious mind, and the quiet member, who later on came with all the wow ideas, is our subconscious mind. As long as our logical and analytical conscious mind is dominant, the subconscious mind remains in the background, quietly connecting the diverse dots, and waiting for a **gap**. The gap comes when the conscious mind stops engaging in the problem.

The gap is where the magic happens.

The above analogy beautifully explains how our subconscious mind works.

Those of you who have a more scientific bent of mind would demand more than just an analogy. If you are one among them, you are in for a treat. In this chapter, with the help of some solid scientific evidence, you will understand what exactly happens inside our brain during such eureka moments.

Understanding the science behind epiphany will be of great help when we move to the next chapters.

The neuroscience behind the aha moments

Where does a flash of insights come from?

What happens inside the brain when a person solves the problem with a flash of insight or the "aha! moment"?

Are the neural paths for insight solution and non-insight solution the same?

To find answers for the above and many more questions, two eminent psychologists, John Kounios from Drexel University and Mark Beeman from Northwestern University, joined hands. They carried out their experiments using EEG – Electroencephalography and fMRI – Functional Magnetic Resonance Imaging.

(To know all the fascinating details about this experiment and for some deep insights, you can read the book[1]—_The Eureka Factor: Creative Insights and The Brain_ by John Kounios and Mark Beeman.)

In the experiment, participants were asked to solve different types of puzzles. Participants were asked to press a button as soon as they thought of a solution to record the exact time when the answer was found. Investigators then correlated the time with the observations on fMRI and EEG machine to understand whether the answer had come to them suddenly, like a flash of insight, or if they used a systematic trial-and-error approach.

The fMRI showed a corresponding increase in blood flow in the part of the brain's right temporal lobe involved in making connections between distantly related ideas. This activity was not present when the word problems were solved analytically.

Simply speaking, the thought process that leads to aha moments or insights involves different parts of the brain compared to the solutions arrived at through analytical thinking.

There is something even more interesting. As observed in the EEG machine, there was a burst of EEG gamma waves in the right hemisphere at the *'aha moment'*. This is not surprising considering that gamma waves are associated with heightened alertness. What surprised them was that the EEG recorded a bust of alpha wave activity about a second before that.

This finding is extremely significant.

Gamma waves indicate the state of intense concentration, whereas alpha waves represent the state of restfulness. How can there be a state of restfulness amid intense concentration? The possible explanation is that just before the insight or aha moments, a burst of alpha waves brings a **gap** or **wandering of the mind**, resulting in a conducive state in the brain for the "*Eureka moment*" to happen.

For long, alpha brain waves had been associated with creative thinking. Alpha brain waves appear to be key to bring creative ideas from the depth of the subconscious mind to the surface of the conscious mind.

In this study conducted in 2015, researchers found clear evidence that enhancing alpha brain waves resulted in a surge in creativity. [2]

Coming back to the wandering mind, you may be wondering, what has it got to do with the *aha moments*?

The wandering mind makes novel connections

According to a study published here, the wandering mind makes more creative connections between completely different sets of dots. These dots are already present in our minds but present in different frames.[3]

A wandering mind is not an empty mind

According to cognitive neuroscientist Kalina Christoff at the University of British Columbia in Vancouver, *"mind wandering is a much more active state than we ever imagined, much more active than during reasoning with a complex problem."*

She has co-authored a book – *The Oxford Handbook of Spontaneous Thought: Mind-Wandering, Creativity, and Dreaming*[4].

I also recommend you look at this article written by Robert Lee Hotz – A Wandering Mind Heads Straight Toward Insight[5].

In the next chapter, you will understand how your subconscious mind can bring creative magic into your life.

Exercise

The main difference between the exercises from this section and the others is that you have to keep doing these exercises even after reading this book. Tuning your subconscious mind to make it your trusted ally in the idea generation process takes practice. Hence, these exercises should become part of your daily routine.

The Happy Reminder

When was the last time you had a creative idea or inspiration to do something different?

What were you thinking then?

What exact activity were you involved in?

Was your mind wandering?

Try to remember it as exactly and as vividly as you can.

Write it down.

Express your gratitude towards your subconscious mind for all the great ideas it has given you in the past.

The reward of doing this exercise will be a happy reminder and reassurance that your subconscious mind is very much active and always trying to help you with creative ideas.

References

1. https://www.amazon.com/Eureka-Factor-Creative-Insights-Brain-ebook/dp/B00RKX0SAC/ref=tmm_kin_swatch_0?_encoding=UTF8&qid=&sr=
2. https://www.sciencedirect.com/science/article/abs/pii/S0010945215001033?via%3Dihub
3. https://journals.sagepub.com/doi/abs/10.1177/0956797612446024
4. https://www.amazon.com/Oxford-Handbook-Spontaneous-Thought-Mind-Wandering-ebook-dp-B07CZM7GZJ/dp/B07CZM7GZJ/ref=mt_other?_encoding=UTF8&me=&qid=
5. https://www.wsj.com/articles/SB124535297048828601

Chapter 13 — *Let The Magic Begin*

"The notes I handle no better than many pianists. But the pauses between the notes ah, that is where the art resides."

- Artur Schnabel

I had mentioned this earlier. I will do so again.

The gap is where the magic happens.

While your logical or analytical mind is at work, in the background, your subconscious mind is quietly working. In the previous chapter, you have seen the scientific evidence on how wow ideas come to the surface when a gap happens. You already know that in order to get wow ideas, you need to connect a completely different set of dots. This is exactly what a wandering mind does. Your strategy, therefore, should be to allow your mind to wander consciously from time to time to create those gaps where the magic will happen.

But here, the wandering mind is not equivalent to idle daydreaming that most people do. You need to follow an effective sequence. Here is the formula to get the most out of your subconscious mind.

Intense focus and let go

Intense focus

The first step is to think hard about the challenge at hand. This is where you will consciously apply your learning from the previous chapter. I hope you remember everything. For your benefit, let me list down all the things you will consciously do during the stage of intense focus.

- Identifying and challenging assumptions.
- Asking different sets of questions to reframe the challenge.
- Searching for different frames.
- Adding more dots in each of the frames.

The purpose of the intense focus is to feed your conscious mind with all possible raw material. This way, you are giving your subconscious mind a chance to come up with completely different connections.

In a majority of books, this process is referred to as immersion. I prefer the term intense focus because I feel that the term immersion lacks the 'intensity' of the efforts and 'the razor-like focus' that you are expected to bring. The term intense focus has immersion inbuilt into it, plus the intensity and the focus.

I want you to try so hard to *make your creative muscle sweat*!

Once you have done that, you are ready to let go.

Let go

If you have read a few books or articles on creativity, I am sure you have come across one of the important phases in the idea generation process: **incubation**. The incubation phase is where you hand over your creative challenge to your subconscious mind. But how to ensure that incubations would result in *aha! moments* with a fair degree of certainty?

There are many ways to let go after the intense focus. I will cover some of them in the next chapter, "Make the subconscious mind your powerful ally". In this chapter, we will focus on **sleep** as a powerful way to bring creative ideas to the surface from the depths of your subconscious.

Sleep on a problem and dream up a solution

August Kekulé had been struggling to figure out how the atoms in benzene are arranged.

While thinking about the problem, he dozed off to sleep.

In his dream, he saw atoms dancing. Gradually the atoms arranged themselves in a long row and started moving about like a snake. As he watched the snake dance, it turned around a bit its own tail.

When Kekulé woke up, he immediately realized the meaning of his dream.

Benzene molecules are made up of rings of carbon atoms.

There are many such stories wherein inventors, in their dream state, were presented with the most critical missing link of the puzzle that they were struggling to solve. This eventually led to many path-breaking inventions.

But the problem is most of us don't remember our dreams. Sometimes we get the sensation of having seen something in the dream. But it is so fragile that it simply disappears within a few seconds. So, even if we are presented with the breakthrough solution through our dream, it is very unlikely that we will remember it.

Here are a few steps that you can carry out to ensure that you find a solution to your problem in the dream and remember the whole dream.

1. Before going to bed, keep a paper and pen ready. Just before drifting off to sleep, mentally say this to yourself, "I want to remember a dream, and I am going to remember a dream." (This I learned from Silva Method of Mind Control. I will talk more about it in a short while.)
2. You will wake up after a dream. Immediately grab your pen and paper and note it down. Practice it for a few days.
3. Once you are satisfied that you can remember your dreams, it's now time to take up your challenge in hand. Bring about the intense focus, the way I have described earlier.

4. This time, just before sleep, say, "I want to have a dream that will contain the solution to the problem that I have in my mind, and I am going to remember it". Most likely, you will see the solution in the dream. Write it down.

Some of you may think it a little far-fetched. Just try it out. Be a little patient, and you will be surprised with the results.

After sleep

Creative people have always known – sleep enhances their creativity. So, whenever they get stuck with a problem, they leave it there and revisit it the next morning. On many occasions, they could quickly solve it by using some creative angle.

In an interesting experiment led by Jan Born of the University of Lübeck, the investigators gave the participants a math problem that they were supposed to solve using a simple rule. However, there was a hidden shortcut that allowed them to arrive at the final answer almost immediately.

Around 25% of the subject discovered the hidden shortcut on their own.

In a group of volunteers who tackled the problem in the evening and returned after eight hours' sleep, the number of people in the group who spotted the shortcut jumped to **more than double**.

Whereas another group who tried the problem in the morning and then spent a normal eight hours of the day awake were just as bad at spotting the trick as those who had stayed awake all night.

The mind that is fresh after sleep is more receptive to the ideas from the subconscious mind.

I have experienced this several times. There have been several instances where I struggled to crack an idea for hours and finally went to bed feeling somewhat worried about missing the client's deadline. The next morning I go through my work in progress, and ideas start flowing. Everything seems to have become so easy. In minutes, so many ideas are cracked!

In 'half-asleep' or 'half-awake' state

Salvador Dali, well known for his surrealist paintings, invented a method he called *"Slumber with a key"*.

During the afternoon, Dali would sit on a chair with a key in his hand. Beneath the key, he would keep a plate arranged upside down. Then he would let himself drift off to sleep. The moment he was about to fall asleep, the key dropped from his hand and fell on the plate. The noise of the key falling on the plate would awaken him, often with artistic ideas.

This fraction of the second long phase between sleeping and wakefulness, which scientists call hypnagogia (from the Greek Hypnos 'sleep' +

agōgos 'leading', or, leading to sleep), is similar to REM sleep. In this state, the mind is fluid and makes creative connections between seemingly remote ideas that may never happen in the wakeful state. In other words, this is a more fertile state to connect unrelated dots that brings a new wow idea.

Hypnagogia had been a subject of interest among psychologists. In 1983, a doctoral thesis written by Andreas Mavromatis was the first landmark work that explained the phenomenon and triggered the interest in its creative potential.

In the previous chapter, while reading about a landmark study by John Kounios and Mark Beeman, you came across alpha brain waves and gamma brain waves. Now let me briefly explain the different types of waves that our brain produces.

Our brain transmits different types of frequencies depending upon the individual's conscious state, which can be measured using EEG. During the wakeful state, we emit prominently beta waves. In a relaxed state, we emit a slower alpha wave. Theta waves are even slower, characterized by drowsiness and the onset of REM sleep. Delta brain waves are the slowest that represent deep sleep, whereas gamma brain waves are the fastest that represent heightened alertness or concentration.

The state of hypnagogia is marked by a high level of both alpha and theta brain waves. In this stage, the individual feels "half-asleep" or "half-awake," and is transiting from wakefulness towards sleep.

The Eureka Factor

In the previous chapter, I mentioned the book co-authored by John Kounios. He was struggling to come up with a title for his book. One late night his wife, while thinking about it, fell asleep. She was awakened with an idea that jolted her during her sleep.

"I have found the title for the book," she informed John.

Her suggestion for the title was "The Eureka Factor".

Finally, at the end of this chapter, I want to clarify something.

It is not necessary that you need to sleep over the problem every time as a part of your 'let go' strategy. At times, during intense focus, for a few seconds or a fraction of a second, try and let go. This will be good enough to get a wow idea. There are more ways to let go. You will learn them in the next chapter. As you keep practicing, you will start effortlessly oscillating between intense focus and let go.

Exercises

1
Intense focus and let go

From this chapter, please once again read through the section on "intense focus" and "let go". Try it out on a challenge that you are working upon. If, at present, you are not working on any challenge, apply it to the challenges pertaining to your most important goal.

2
Remember your dreams

From this chapter, apply the technique to remember a dream. Do it every day before going to bed.

3
Find the solution in your dream

Once you start remembering your dreams, apply the technique given in this chapter to find the solution to your challenges in the dream.

4
After sleep

Revisit your challenge, and take stock of so many frames you have created since you started working on it. Can you think of more angles? Work on it just before going to sleep. The next day, give a fresh look at all the work you did the previous night.

Did you get any new angles to your challenge?

Chapter 14 — *Make The Subconscious Mind Your Powerful Ally*

During your childhood, you must have read a folk tale of Aladdin and the magic lamp. As the tale goes, a genie, the slave of the lamp, would appear when Aladdin rubbed the magic lamp. His first words would be, "Master, your wish is my command." After that, whatever Aladdin demands, the genie will fulfill it.

Is the subconscious mind like a genie, the slave of the lamp, who could grant you any wish?

Yes and no.

Yes, because, like a genie, the subconscious mind has the power to find the creative solution to almost every problem.

No, because you can never make your subconscious mind your slave.

Try nailing the subconscious mind to a nine to five job; it won't work. On the contrary, the subconscious mind loves to present the most creative solutions to you at the most unexpected hours.

So, isn't there any way to get the best out of your subconscious mind? Yes, there is. Understand how the subconscious mind works and change your approach accordingly.

Here, I would like to clarify something – The power of the subconscious mind can impact so many aspects of your life, and a lot is already written about it. But for this book, I have discussed the subconscious mind only in the context of creativity.

The subconscious mind responds to your belief about creative ability

For your subconscious mind, your belief about your creative ability is the command. And it will faithfully go on to make your command a reality.

Do you keep saying things like this?

"I am not an idea person."

"I am not exactly the creative type."

"Somehow, creativity is not my cup of tea."

"Creativity can't be learned. Only a few people are born with it."

"My ideas may sound stupid."

"What if people laugh at my ideas?"

"Ideas are a dime a dozen."

"I don't believe in ideas. After all, it's execution that matters."

You may not be using exact words or phrases. But you got the idea. By believing that you are not creative, you are sending negative affirmations to your subconscious mind. Your subconscious mind will respond accordingly.

Hence, the first action is to believe that you are creative and start telling your subconscious mind the same.

How would you communicate with your subconscious mind? Through affirmations. You can use the below affirmations to create a new set of belief systems.

I practice new thinking all the time.

I look at things differently.

Creative ideas come easily and effortlessly. I can generate ideas on demand.

I love thinking outside the box.

I generate multiple creative solutions for every challenge.

I create opportunities out of every challenge.

My creative ideas are in demand. Those around me appreciate my unique gift of creativity.

Affirmations will give you a good start. But there are still more things to be done.

The subconscious mind responds to your trust

Your subconscious mind expects trust and encouragement. One way your subconscious mind knows how much you trust it is through your actions. Here comes the difficult part. On many occasions, some of the ideas that come from your subconscious mind may seem to you quite impractical, illogical, or farfetched. Your first impulse will be to reject them. But soon, you will discover that the more often you reject, the less often you will get new ideas.

The best policy is to pursue those ideas further, however illogical they sound in the beginning. Soon some dots will begin to get connected. And before you realize it, your problem is cracked.

Let me share my personal experience.

There are occasions when ideas start flowing in my head as soon as a client starts briefing. I bounce a few of them off the client to get the buy-in. I love to see the surprise on the client's face when he realizes that the challenge is already cracked! Something he had been struggling with for days or even months.

But there are occasions when exactly the opposite happens.

When I hear the briefing from the client, I am completely clueless. I start feeling that the client is expecting me to pull a rabbit out of the hat.

I am stuck; I struggle a lot. During the team brainstorming, we try to look at the challenge in different ways. We end up brainstorming with the feeling that we are miles away from cracking the challenge. Perhaps we need many more rounds of brainstorming. Our timelines seem to be going haywire. I start feeling somewhat worried. And then, when I am involved in some mundane activity, not thinking about the work, comes suddenly the *aha! moment*. The dots are connected unexpectedly. The ideas are cracked!

This idea was a completely new angle that I had never thought of. It was presented to me on a platter.

I present my idea to the client. The client is thrilled. My reputation as a creative guy remains unscratched.

To be honest, I know one thing – This was not my idea. I didn't crack it for sure. Because I didn't ARRIVE at this breakthrough idea through my step-by-step thinking. It just happened as if some outsider had put it in my mind. I even silently express my gratitude to that unknown entity who gifted me with the right ideas at the right time.

As I started going deep into creativity, I understood that it is the subconscious mind at work.

But why has the subconscious mind been so generous with me? It's simply due to my years of practice. I have created a conducive environment for the subconscious mind to help me effortlessly, most of the time.

Besides, I have started completely trusting my subconscious mind. I have experienced that the more I trust it, the more favorably it responds.

During all such episodes, one factor had always been quite consistent. The dots got connected **when my mind was wandering**.

Allow your mind to wander

Bertrand Russell wrote in *The Conquest of Happiness: "I have found, for example, that, if I have to write upon some rather difficult topic, the best plan is to think about it with very great intensity — the greatest intensity of which I am capable — for a few hours or days, and at the end of that time give orders, so to speak, that the work is to proceed underground. After some months, I return consciously to the topic and find that the work has been done."*

The productivity freaks will urge you not to let your mind wander even for a minute. But creativity is different. It operates on a different set of rules.

In the words of J, R. R. Tolkien, *"Not all those who wander are lost."*

When the wandering mind comes back, it brings along many gold nuggets.

Analytical problem solving needs intense focus. Creative idea generation requires focus, followed by moments of distraction. Hence, if you are stuck despite the intense effort during ideation, consciously distract your mind into something completely different and mundane. This distraction or wandering of the mind will create a gap, allowing your subconscious mind to bring a free flow of creative ideas. Even those activities that bring momentary physical relaxation can bring a flood of ideas from your subconscious mind. Many people sheepishly admit that some of their best ideas have come to them during the biological break. I tell them that there is no need to feel sheepish and assure them that I am also part of the same league. There are countless people who experience a flood of creative ideas while having a shower. Unlike the previous set of people, these people don't mind being vocal about it.

"Why do I always get my best ideas in the shower?"

- Albert Einstein

Go out for a walk

The Stanford study published in 2014 found that walking improved creativity output by 60 percent. According to the study researcher, "Walking opens up the free flow of ideas."

This study only confirmed what creative brains already knew.

Charles Darwin used to go for a walk two times a day. Steve Jobs used to prefer to carry out brainstorming meetings while walking with his colleagues.

How does walking improve your creativity? It does in more ways than one.

Walking improves your mood. A happy mood brings your brain to a state that is conducive to creativity. Earlier, I have mentioned research work carried out by John Kounios. According to

Kounios, a mind that is in a happy state is more likely to get creative ideas.

Now there is an interesting twist! [Recent research](#) indicates that exercise enhances creativity, independent of your mood. So, surely walking improves creativity in more than one way.

Many creative minds had discovered their *aha! moments*, when they went for a long walk after focusing hard, for long hours on the challenge they were trying to crack. This tells us that after **intense focus**, walking brings us to the state of **let go**, where the subconscious mind takes over.

I mentioned earlier about the wandering mind. Walking, like having a shower, relaxes us. This relaxation distracts our focused minds. Our subconscious mind uses this gap created by the wandering mind as a window of opportunity to bring ideas to the surface. As put by a Stanford study researcher, "Walking opens up the free flow of ideas." The researchers further found that walking helps in divergent thinking, helps us in connecting the diverse dots. At the beginning of this book, I had mentioned people with a *The Right Answer* mindset. These people are largely engaged in convergent thinking. With such thinking, researchers observed that walking offers no additional benefit.

Reading

Books have greatly impacted my life. I consider myself fortunate for having come across the right books at the right stage of my life. Whatever I have achieved in my life, both personally and professionally, books have played a major role.

Before the start of my professional career, a set of books helped me to build my self-esteem. At the beginning of my career, I understood the framework of success by reading some great books. Later, I discovered one benefit of books – getting creative ideas. Here, I want to state that the creative ideas that struck me while reading books play a large role in shaping my professional success.

What is your experience? Did you experience some eureka moments while reading books? By now, you have got a fairly good hang of the role of the subconscious mind in getting the wow ideas. Next time you read a new book, read a blog post, watch a video, listen to a podcast, or do anything that can put you in a creative flow, do it with a clear intention of igniting your creativity. While reading a book, you may start experiencing some vague sensation about ideas from your subconscious mind trying to come up to the surface. Don't suppress it. Stop reading, listening, or whatever you are doing and try to listen to your subconscious. Initially, you may have to do it consciously. But at a later stage, so many ideas will start rushing to your mind that you will be forced to rush for your pen and pad.

I have a huge collection of physical books. In the past several years, I have bought perhaps an equal number of eBooks. After some deep work, I sometimes take a break and select a book from my collection that I feel like picking up by simply following my intuition. After selecting a book, I randomly open a page, expecting to find something valuable. On many occasions, I am not disappointed. I find something that I can directly or indirectly connect with the project that I am working on.

Express gratitude as often as you can

Energy follows thought. If you find yourself complaining often, what are you focusing on? The lack. You will get more of it. Similarly, when you express gratitude towards something. What is that you are grateful about? The things that you have. The more gratitude you express in a day, and every day, the more abundance will come into your life.

The same holds good about your subconscious mind. Whenever you get any spark of an idea, if judging the idea has been your default mode, replace it with gratitude. Express your gratitude towards your subconscious mind. Don't hold it for the breakthrough idea. The more grateful you are towards your subconscious mind, and the more often you express it, the more wow ideas it will bring for you.

Practice meditation

In chapter 12, we saw that John Kounios and Mark Beeman observed a burst of alpha activity just before the *aha! moment*. In the same chapter, I referred to one more study that offers clear evidence that enhancing alpha brain waves results in a surge in creativity.

Our brain produces alpha waves just before you drift into sleep and just after you wake up.

Since alpha brain waves are so strongly related to creative ideas, won't it be great if we can create alpha brain waves on demand to generate ideas on demand?

Yes, you can. I mean, you can do both. This book is about generating **ideas on demand**. Coming to creating alpha waves on-demand, you can do it through meditation. I have experienced it. I attended a Silva mind control workshop way back in the nineties. I found the Silva method to be quite effective in helping attain alpha brain frequency. I do not doubt that it has helped me come up with creative ideas. In addition to creativity, alpha brain frequency has many other benefits in our day-to-day life. I strongly recommend learning more about it by reading the book – *The Silva Mind Control Method* by Jose Silva.

Write down your ideas

As you will become proficient in harnessing the power of your subconscious mind, ideas will start flowing effortlessly. Here, I must caution you that these ideas are extremely fragile. At that moment, you may feel confident that you will remember every single idea. But within a few moments, they are gone. Due to their fragility, I must have lost countless ideas. Having learned my lesson the hard way, I try to deploy every possible way to capture them as soon as they start pouring out of my head.

I strongly recommend you plan ways to capture your ideas. They may pop up at any time. In the car, in the shower, while taking a long walk, as soon as you wake up in the morning or when you suddenly wake up in the middle of the night and realize that your subconscious mind has brought a big wow idea for you.

While having a walk, keep your mobile recorder handy. While traveling, you may want to use some mobile app to key in the ideas quickly. I still find great value in old-fashioned pen and pad. I keep them scattered all over the place.

For creative inspiration, Beethoven used to take long solitary walks through the countryside. He always made it a point to carry a pencil and paper to record every inspiring idea.

There is something more.

The subconscious mind does something more – It can cause accidents in your life.

Don't look alarmed

What I am referring to are happy accidents. Let's move on to the next chapter.

Exercises

1

Affirmations

Repeat the positive affirmations given in this chapter. Keep doing it every day. Over a period of time, this will help you to change your self-belief.

2

Trust your subconscious mind

Learning to trust your subconscious mind happens in two steps.

1. Listen to your subconscious mind: Subconscious mind always tries to tell us something. We are either too busy to take notice or don't recognize it as an idea from our subconscious mind and brush it aside, thinking it be some stupid idea. This exercise is something that you have to keep doing all the time. Start carefully watching your thoughts. Try to figure out whether they are from your conscious mind or subconscious mind. Thoughts from your conscious mind are logical, linear, and closely related to the matter you are thinking about. Whereas the thoughts coming from your subconscious mind may appear to you as unconnected, illogical, irrational, and at times outright shocking. Start noting down all those thoughts even if they don't make any sense to you. Over time,

you will easily learn to identify the voice of your subconscious mind.
2. The second part is a somewhat difficult one. It involves going by all the "unconnected, illogical, irrational, and at times outright shocking" coming from your subconscious mind. Start with the simple things. Let's say you are busy with some work, and at that time, the thought of calling someone comes to your mind. Your logical mind will have every reason not to make that call. But go ahead and make the call. Or you may feel like opening some book for no particular reason. Don't suppress that thought. Go ahead and open it. Initially, don't expect any breakthrough to happen. By following such thoughts, you are telling your subconscious mind that you are trusting it.

3

Expressing gratitude

Before retiring in the night, think of all the small or big ideas that you could think of. Express your gratitude toward your subconscious mind for every idea. It's possible during the initial days you can't remember any, still be grateful, generally. Do it for a few days, and you will notice that you will start finding a few ideas to be grateful for every night.

4

Practice other techniques

Besides allowing your mind to wander, practice other techniques mentioned in the chapter like going out for a walk, reading, and meditation. You might be already doing a few of these things. But henceforth, you will do them while being conscious about the thoughts that come to your mind while doing the above activities.

5

Maintain an idea book

Get a nice notebook. Keep it always with you. Call it an "I" book or by whatever you may like. Whenever an idea comes to your mind, note it down. Don't judge and discard any of the ideas. These are all dots. You never know; in the future, they may connect with other dots and form valuable gems.

I started this practice after moving from sales to marketing. Initially, the quality of my ideas was pathetic. But I persisted. With time, ideas started getting better. I am immensely benefited by it.

References

1. https://www.amazon.com/Conquest-Happiness-Bertrand-Russell-dp-1684116694/dp/1684116694/ref=mt_other?_encoding=UTF8&me=&qid= https://www.researchgate.net/publication/261768023_Give_Your_Ideas_Some_Legs_The_Positive_Effect_of_Walking_on_Creative_Thinking
2. https://www.ncbi.nlm.nih.gov/pmc/articles/PMC1332529/
3. https://www.amazon.com/Silva-Mind-Control-Method/dp/0671739891/ref=sr_1_1?dchild=1&keywords=The+Silva+Mind+Control+Method+Mass+Market+Paperback&qid=1621625614&s=books&sr=1-1

Chapter 15 — *Serendipity: Revel In Happy Accidents*

"A lot of it, as it is in any job in life, is being in the right place at the right time."

- Julie Harris

Once you follow the steps mentioned previously, you will be well-tuned with your subconscious mind. Once that happens, you are more likely to find yourself in the right place at the right time. Your subconscious mind will bring many happy accidents in your life, which is known as **serendipity**.

We saw earlier, Archimedes tried hard, but he was stuck. Finally, he decided that his mind needed a break. He could have helped himself with a cup of hot coffee, or he could have straightway headed towards a pub. But those were not the places where Archimedes could find the answer.

Archimedes's subconscious mind led him to the only place where 'Eureka' could happen – a bathtub.

Similarly, when Goodyear had gone completely bankrupt and was desperate for the money. His subconscious mind knew what was needed to create a happy accident – a hot stove.

Charles Goodyear, while demonstrating his experiment, dropped the rubber mixture on a hot stove. It got burnt and finally dried. When Goodyear began to scrape it off, he found that it had become hard but still retained its rubber-like property. He soon realized that heat was the answer in making it more durable. In the process, a new way of transforming natural rubber into a more durable form called vulcanization was invented.

The subconscious mind operates mysteriously. It can make you commit mistakes. Such mistakes can lead to a creative breakthrough. Provided you are ready to spot an opportunity in it.

While conducting research, Alexander Graham Bell came across a book titled Sensations of Tone by Hermann von Helmholtz. Unfortunately, Bell could not understand the book written in German and therefore relied on the accompanying diagrams.

Helmholtz, in his book, had described his experiment stating that vowel sounds can be reproduced by using electric tuning forks. Bell misinterpreted that electrical wire could reproduce vowel sounds. While Bell realized his mistake soon, he did not let go of the possibility of electric transmission of sound. He pursued it further, which eventually resulted in the invention of the telephone.

"In the fields of observation, chance favors only the prepared mind."

- Louis Pasteur

How to make serendipity happen to you more often

Over the years, I have come to one conclusion. Serendipity is not just happy accidents that *happen* to some lucky people. It is something that you can *attract* into your life.

Here are five techniques for turning yourself into a serendipity magnet:

1. Follow your intuition

As I had said earlier, the subconscious mind operates in its own mysterious way. You need to surrender to it and allow it to guide you.

It is difficult. Certain events, thoughts, or actions at that time won't make you any sense. At times, it even seems like the wrong thing to do. As in the case of Bell, there was a mistake on Bell's part in translating the original German text. But he pursued his "mistake," and the breakthrough happened.

2. Keep researching and keep searching

The history of scientific inventions is full of examples of happy accidents resulting in breakthrough inventions. But you will agree that those were not necessarily the first instances. So, why didn't similar incidences earlier result in eureka moments? The reasons are obvious; for such accidents to translate into breakthroughs, two things are needed—1. A prepared mind with a solid background of knowledge. 2. An alert mind that is constantly seeking the solution.

For everyone, Goodyear's story was an example of a happy accident. But Goodyear vehemently disagreed. He insisted that the stove incidence held meaning only for someone *"whose mind was prepared to draw an inference"* and who had *"applied himself most perseveringly to the subject."*

3. Being at the right place

For serendipity to happen, you need to be at the right place, as randomness is at the heart of serendipity.

Before the accidental discovery of vulcanized rubber, Goodyear was in a financially dire state and was quite desperate to find an investor for his product. He traveled anywhere he could find potential investors to whom he could present his product.

Traveling to unfamiliar places brings you closer to random intersections of ideas.

You don't always have to travel to an unfamiliar place for serendipity to happen. Even being in a place or a conducive environment can foster moments of serendipity. This environment conducive to serendipity was at the back of Steve Job's mind when he conceived Pixar's new building design.

Here is what he said:

"There's a temptation in our networked age to think that ideas can be developed by email and iChat. That's crazy. Creativity comes from spontaneous meetings, from random discussions. You run into someone, you ask what they're doing, you say 'Wow,' and soon you're cooking up all sorts of ideas."

4. Moving out of your comfort zone

Serendipity won't happen by being in the comfort zone of your home or the familiar environment. You need to be ready to get connected to new people, start a conversation with a stranger. Even if the environment is unfamiliar, you need to be ready to show up.

Stef Lewandowski, in this article published in Medium, shares an interesting experience. A few years ago, he was invited to an event, but he had a problem. He narrates, *"The thing is, I was broke. My bank account was empty, and I was down to my last handful of cash. To get to the event, I'd be using it to pay for a train ticket."*

He didn't know what he would find there, but he was quite convinced that it would be a room full of opportunities. He, therefore, decided to go ahead, spending his last penny. During the event, he had a brief chat with someone. Later on, together, they found a new company.

5. Start expecting it

Remember, whatever your mind focuses upon, the energy follows.

When you wake up every day, bring the feeling of expectancy. Start keenly observing all the random events. Ask yourself, "What is this random event trying to communicate to me?"

One way to make it a habit is to keep a journal of "random" things that happen during the day.

Bottom line – expect it every day. Search for it. Write it down. Experience more of it.

Become a "Go-Giver"

When you start enjoying helping others and impacting many lives, you start attracting serendipity in your life.

From the time I started my corporate career, the importance of being a "go-getter" was strongly imbibed in my mind. If you are into sales function, being a go-getter is a must. Later on, I came across a book titled, *[The Go-Giver: A Little Story About a Powerful Business Idea](#)*, written by Bob Burg and John David Mann.

As a creative person, I loved the phrase, "Go-Giver."

As someone who is spiritually inclined, I am a strong believer in the law of karma, and hence the concept of "giving" resonated so much with me.

And I loved the way the whole story was told. I subsequently read all the other books in the series. I strongly recommend that you do the same.

Coming back to serendipity, I noticed that the more I give, the more happy incidents happen in my life.

Are you wondering what happened to the "Go-getter" within me? As I have said earlier, in a creative mind, many "rights" exist. So, for me, these are just two different rights, and perhaps there are more.

In this section, I have tried to cover several aspects of the subconscious mind and how you can unleash its power. Understand it thoroughly, practice the exercises given, make the subconscious mind your trusted ally and enjoy the flood of creative ideas.

Exercises

1
Expecting serendipity

Before you go to bed, affirm that tomorrow your subconscious mind will take you to places, connect with people, or make you stumble upon the things from where you will get ideas or answers that you are searching for.

When you wake up, immediately bring yourself into a state of expectations. Throughout the day, keep keenly looking for serendipity.

Remember, for serendipity to happen, you need an alert mind.

2
Practice giving

Make a resolve to "give" a minimum of one thing every day. It need not always be in the form of money or kind. It could be some useful information that someone is seeking, giving attention, giving a small part of your time to those who need it the most, a bright smile, the list can be unending. Once you keep searching for an opportunity to give, you will keep finding many. Your day's minimum target is one. There is no upper limit.

Be a prolific giver. By giving, you substantially increase your probability of serendipity.

Remember, when you give anything, the universe will return it manifold.

References

1. https://medium.com/makeshift-thoughts/accelerating-serendipity-1d03b0d4da2b
2. https://www.amazon.com/Go-Giver-Little-Story-Powerful-Business-ebook/dp/B003AYZBJI/ref=tmm_kin_s watch_0?_encoding=UTF8&qid=&sr=

Section # 6 - Generating Ideas on Demand

Chapter 16 – *Generating Ideas On Demand*

Anything that is not used for a long period gets atrophied, be it a body muscle, be it an idea muscle.

Luckily, you have stumbled upon this book. And you didn't stop there. You have read it up to this point. Besides, after reading every chapter, you gave your idea muscle a healthy dose of workout. You no longer have to worry about idea muscle atrophy.

If you attempted all the exercises at the end of every chapter, you have already tasted many small doses of success. You must be noticing a clear shift in your belief from "creativity is not my cup of tea" to "I know, I can master creativity."

If that has happened to you, congratulations! You have already crossed many milestones.

Now it's time to achieve massive success. You will do it by facing your ultimate challenge and emerging victorious. So, please apply all your might in cracking the exercise given at the end of the section titled "Your Ultimate Challenge."

Your victory will permanently shift your belief system from "I know, I can master creativity" to "I AM creative." As you will start believing yourself as a creative being, you will start noticing a significant jump in the quality as well as quantity of your ideas.

You will be ready to generate **Ideas on Demand.**

Before you get ready, a "creative booster" awaits you in the next chapter.

Let's move on.

Chapter 17 – *Boost Your Creativity With Constraints*

Imagine you are heading a creative project; you have a world at your disposal. People, technology, expert advice, the ambiance of your choice, any resource you name, you have the budget for it. Isn't it the ideal environment to bring out the best of creativity and innovation?

As it turns out, this kind of freedom can actually be counterproductive.

The key to unleashing creativity is not removing all the constraints but the imposition of some healthy constraints that challenge us to think differently.

Let me share my personal experience.

"Miliind, the big boss has called a meeting on Friday." A client makes a frantic call. "He wants to see all the creative work for the upcoming campaign."

"Don't you think Friday is too short notice?" I protest. "You know, his expectations are always quite high. You need to give us adequate time to come up with the ideas that exceed his expectations."

"It's not possible, Miliind. Please help me this time."

"Okay, we will give it our best shot." I had no other option but to give in to his pleadings.

We were obviously not happy with such unrealistic timelines imposed on us. But as it happened on several occasions in the past, these "unrealistic timelines" brought out some really wow ideas. The client was delighted.

This is not to tell you how exceptionally creative we are. If you speak to creative people from ad agencies, they will tell you that this is how they deliver wow ideas every after day under unrealistic timelines. Not just creative people from ad agencies, all creative ones will vouch for the fact that **constraint of time** brings out the best from them.

You may think that I have narrated to you an exceptional case. No, the above case is not an exception. It's almost like a rule. The "this time" mentioned by the client, keeps happening almost "every time."

Time is just one of the constraints. There are many. As a creative agency, we have experienced almost all of them. As a result, I would say that if you want to sharpen your creativity, constraints are your best friends. I will share some of our other experiences in a short while.

Do you find it hard to believe? After all, creativity needs freedom. You can't pin a creative guy down with constraints and expect him to produce a masterpiece, can you?

When faced with constraints, people have conceived and executed some fascinating ideas.

What do you do when you are stuck at the airport overnight?

Richard Dunn was all alone. He had several hours to kill in deserted Las Vegas airport. He didn't let his situation overpower his mind with boredom and frustration. Instead, he looked for an opportunity. He found one—to create a video that can go viral. But other than his iPhone, he didn't have any other resources. This would have been a reason sufficient enough for others to give up the very idea. But for Dunn, a vast deserted airport was a great resource as an empty movie set.

He created a video lip-synching to Celine Dion's *All By Myself* song. While writing this book, his video had 7.5 million views on Vimeo.

In an interview with CBC/Radio-Canada, he explains how he shot the video all alone. "I then used a wheelchair that had a tall pole on the back of it and taped my iPhone to that. Then I would put it on the moving walkway for a dolly shot. I also used the extended handle on my computer bag and taped the iPhone to my handle."

I had said earlier; creativity is not just for problem-solving, it's for creating new opportunities. Constraints can fast-track you to a new opportunity.

What does the scientific evidence tell us?

In a 2015 study, Ravi Mehta at the University of Illinois and Meng Zhu at Johns Hopkins University examined how thinking about scarcity or abundance influences the way people creatively use their resources. They found that in the situation where resources are in abundance, people simply have no incentive to use the available resources in a creative way. On the other hand, resource scarcity forces people to deploy unconventional ways to use what was available to them[1].

Oguz A. Acar, Murat Tarakci, and Daan van Knippenberg, in the HBR article[2], "Why constraints are good for innovation" while referring to the finding of their study, state, *"We reviewed 145 empirical studies on the effects of constraints on creativity and innovation and found that individuals, teams, and organizations alike benefit from a healthy dose of constraints. It is only when the constraints become too high that they stifle creativity and innovation."*

We have heard stories of startups with limited resources dislodging big established brands with a big marketing budget. Surplus resources make people and organizations comfortable. They tend to do things in conventionally. Only when faced with constraints do people use unconventional ways to use their resources and achieve their objectives because they have to.

That's what Phil did.

Shaking off the constraint

"You have permanent nerve damage," announced the neurologist after doing a thorough examination.

Phil was shaken.

Phil's hand had been shaking, literally, for the past few years.

Phil had an intense desire to become an artist. His single-minded pursuit of pointillism led to tremors in his hand and the ultimate diagnosis of nerve damage.

After looking at the squiggly line drawn by Phil, the neurologist suggested, "Well, why don't you just embrace the shake?"

Phil did. He used his constraint to present this world to completely new forms of art.

I strongly recommend you to watch this Ted talk of the world-recognized artist, speaker, author, and innovator, Phil Hansen[4]. This talk will change the way you look at constraints.

"The more constraints one imposes, the more one frees one's self. And the arbitrariness of the constraint serves only to obtain precision of execution."

- Igor Stravinsky

Why am I grateful for all these constraints?

During my corporate career, I didn't fully realize the critical role that constraints play in bringing out the best of your creativity. I understood it thoroughly and had been experiencing it only after working with many corporate clients from the other side of the table.

As a creative communication agency, we work with clients from the pharmaceutical industry. It's commonly believed that communication from pharmaceutical companies to HCPs (doctors) must be loaded with hard science. Besides, you might be aware, it's a highly regulated industry. Every piece of communication that gets out of the company has to pass the scrutiny of different functions like medical, regulatory, and compliance. This leaves very little space for creativity. Many marketing and advertising professionals from other industries simply dismiss it as something too unattractive for their creative ability. In this scenario, clients expect us to bring a wow through creative communication despite the **constraint of regulation.**

We know one thing. If we hate it and keep complaining about it, this mindset will stop us from being creative. We have only one choice—to consider it as a creative challenge. Keep producing wow ideas, so clients keep coming back to us.

We work with all sizes of companies, small, medium, and large. Based on the size of the company and brand, their budget varies. Sometimes we have the luxury to work with a big promotional budget, sometimes it's tight. There have been occasions when we felt that the budget was ridiculously low. Interestingly, some of our best campaigns were conceived when we had to work under **resource constraints.**

Different clients we work for have different tastes and preferences. We have to work under those constraints. When our work is presented to the top bosses, they have a completely different point of view. That brings us the **constraint of limited options**. Besides, every organization has its corporate brand guidelines. Our designers have to work under those constraints. The copywriter has to work within the **constraint of words**.

Does the constraint of words hamper creativity? It doesn't seem so.

Constraints can help you win a bet

As the legend goes, Ernest Hemingway was having lunch with his friends, and the discussion moved on to the subject of brevity. Hemingway claimed that he could write a six-word story that could make people cry. His friends strongly contested this claim. He challenged them to bet $10. He then wrote on a paper napkin, "For sale: baby shoes, never worn."

This is a classic example of how the mind can bring out the best of creative ideas when put under constraint.

Let me introduce you to one more constraint. I started the introduction of this book with a quote that stated that 10x is easier than 10 percent. When the set expectations are low, we tend to rely on the past and try to get results by doing the same things "more" or "better". But when we commit ourselves to an audacious goal, we realize that the incremental approach won't work. We need to do something dramatically "different." In a way, we create a constraint for ourselves. This constraint forces us to take a departure from the linear approach and take a lateral route. This is how the **constraint of high aspirational goals** brings out our creativity.

This was one reason why I was urging you to aim for an audacious goal during your first exercise.

Covid 19 has imposed constraints on us that we had never imagined. Face-to-face meetings and events have taken a back seat. We all have stories of countless people losing their jobs and businesses closing down during this global pandemic. At the same time, we have also witnessed individuals and organizations displaying an unprecedented level of adaptability, agility, and creativity. A few coaches, trainers, and consultants I know have figured out ways to move on to the digital platform and access the global market. In contrast, many more are still lamenting about lost business due to this **environmental constraint**.

Working under constraints is a sure way to make your idea muscle sweat, make it stronger, and boost your creativity.

References

1. https://vimeo.com/97634383
2. https://www.cbc.ca/shift/2014/06/10/all-by-himself-at-las-vegas-airport/
3. https://academic.oup.com/jcr/article-abstract/42/5/767/1855952
4. https://hbr.org/2019/11/why-constraints-are-good-for-innovation
5. https://journals.sagepub.com/doi/full/10.1177/0149206318805832?journalCode=joma
6. https://www.youtube.com/watch?v=YrZTho_o_is

Chapter 18 — *Become the Idea Machine*

A critical step to out-of-the-box thinking is finding new boxes or frames.

You have already learned the way to find new frames by changing your questions. Now I am going to share another powerful technique, with examples, which is known as the **random words technique**.

But before I proceed, even at the cost of repetition, I would like to summarize some of the **most important key learning** from previous chapters to set the context. Please read them carefully.

1. People struggle with creativity because they tend to connect the same set of dots and, therefore, end up getting the same run-of-the-mill ideas.
2. A wow idea happens when you connect completely diverse dots the way no one has ever done.
3. To be able to make such connections, you need lots of dots as well as different types of dots.
4. To get both the above, you need to look for different frames.
5. Your assumptions are the invisible barriers that stop you from seeing beyond your existing frames.

6. Questions that you ask determine in which frame answers will fall. If you keep asking the same set of questions, you will keep struggling inside the same frame.
7. Changing your questions is a powerful way to **i.** Break the invisible barrier of assumptions **ii.** Discover new frames.

I hope every point mentioned above is crystal clear to you. If not, please read them once again.

All the learning that I have summarized in **seven bullet points** plus the **random words technique** that I am going to share and **all the exercises** given in this book are sufficient to make you **an idea machine**.

Random words technique

This technique starts with selecting a random word. The random word is a completely new dot. In my experience, on most occasions, the random word doesn't connect directly with your challenge or your dot. To bring about the connections, you need to find a set of **connecting words** to the random word.

Let me show you, with the **examples of different random words,** different ways to **find multiple connecting words**:

<u>Immediate recall</u>

The word that immediately strikes you after hearing the random word.

Example — Random word: puncture; Immediate recall: needle

<u>Strongly associated word</u>

Example— Random word: game; Associated word: basketball

<u>Synonyms</u>

Example— Random word: drive; Synonyms: push, power, ride, desire; Here, different synonyms belong to different frames.

You can further increase your connected words by looking for synonyms of strongly associated words or words related to functionality.

<u>Opposites</u>

Example—Random word: organized; Opposite: haphazard

<u>Related to the functionality</u>

Example—Random word: pen; Function: writing

<u>Parts or the components</u>

Example—Random word: wristwatch; Parts or the components: stripe, dial, hands, button cell

<u>Related to attributes</u>

Example—Random word: tortoise; Attribute: slow

<u>Derived from the associated phrase</u>

Example—Random word: ice; Phrase: cut no ice – connecting words – impressed or unimpressed

I hope you got the hang of it. You can think of more approaches to get the connecting words. There need not be any hard and fast rule. Here, the objective is to arrive at the maximum number of new words.

You can **connect** the connecting words **directly with your challenge** and also use them to **create new frames**.

Let me explain all the steps involved, with an example of a hypothetical situation.

Situation

You are a business consultant, and a client approaches you to seek your professional advice. He is struggling to add new customers and also to retain the existing ones. He had tried doing "more" and "better" of what he had been doing. However, it doesn't seem to be working for him. He wants to hear a completely new set of ideas from you.

Step 1

Choosing a random word

You can pick up any book and randomly open a page and without reading its content, keep your finger on any of the words. That's your random word.

Alternatively, go to Google. Type "random word generator" in a search box. You will get plenty of options. Select any one of them and generate your random word.

For this example, I found out my random word using the first method. The random word that I got is **"bicycle."**

Now, the first thought that may come to your mind is, how can one connect the random word, bicycle, with the situation described above? As I mentioned earlier, such connections rarely happen in the first instance. Hence, we go to the next step.

Step 2

Choosing a connecting word

I have already explained, with examples, different methods to arrive at the connecting word. Now, let's apply those methods to our random word, bicycle, to find a new set of connecting words.

Immediate recall words

After seeing bicycle as a random word, the words that immediately came to my mind were – ride, cyclic, skill, and balance.

Synonyms

I picked up one of the connecting words, ride, and looked for synonyms, and arrived at the word, journey.

Parts or the components

Wheels

Alignment (of all the components)

<u>Related to attributes</u>

Speed

<u>Google autocomplete</u>

The autocomplete feature of Google is another useful way of finding tons of connecting words. Go to Google search, enter your random word, press a space bar, and enter an alphabet. A dropdown window will suggest words that are commonly searched along with your random word.

Here are examples of a few useful connecting words that I found using this method.

Bicycle a → Bicycle accessories

Accessories

Bicycle b → Bicycle bell

Bell

Bicycle j → Bicycle jersey

Jersey

Now with this method, we have a bank of twelve words (dots).

Step 3

This step involves **connecting these dots** with the client's challenge. In the process, **new frames** will get created. Let's see how many frames we can create.

Cyclic → Cyclic nature of the business

Most businesses are cyclic in nature. During the year, there are peak months as well as lean months. Every business knows its lean period. Can the client think of a strategy to acquire new customers specific to the lean period? The other option could be to utilize the lean period to strengthen the relationship with the existing customers.

1. **Frame**—Season specific promotion
2. **Frame**—Strengthening customer relationship

Journey→ Customer journey

Very broadly speaking, customer journey tells us different touchpoints wherein customer interacts with your brand. Organizations design their processes and systems around these touchpoints to create a better customer experience. Does such a system exist in the client's organization?

3. **Frame**—Processes and systems

Skills

Cycling needs skill. The organization should critically look at key positions and do a skill gap analysis. Based on the gaps identified, plan for customized training intervention.

4. **Frame**—Learning and development

Balance

While a company goes overboard on acquiring new customers, they need to balance new customer acquisition and retain and delight their existing customers.

5. **Frame**—Prioritizations

Wheels

Is the company always trying to reinvent the wheel? Instead of trying to figure out new approaches for customer acquisition, it can take a close look at the basics, figure out the lacunae and focus on becoming strong in basics.

6. **Frame**—Processes and systems (existing)

Speed

How fast a company responds to customer's queries or concerns. Can they map the present Turn Around Time (TAT) and find ways to reduce it further and bring about customer delight?

7. **Frame**—Customer delight

Different parts of the bicycle

The bicycle runs smoothly when all its parts are functioning properly and also aligned optimally. Similarly, to bring about customer delight, not just sales and marketing, the support functions have a role to play as well. Are all the functions fully aligned? Do the support functions are also fully committed to bringing about customer delight?

8. **Frame**—Teamwork

Accessories

Many products also market accessories around their brands. If the customer also buys accessories with the main product, they can earn extra money from the same customer. For example, when you are making an online purchase of a laptop, accessories like a keyboard, mouse, laptop screen show up when the customer reviews the cart before paying.

Can the client think of building a product range of accessories around its mainstream product?

9. **Frame**—Business per customer

Bell

From the word bell, I was reminded of an alarm bell or the early warning indicators.

Unless some robust system exists, complaints or dissatisfaction won't reach the company's top leadership. If this continues, the organization keeps steadily losing its customers. In the client's organization, does a system exist that raises the alarm, which draws the attention of all concerned, as and when the customer expresses the slightest dissatisfaction?

10. **Frame**—Minimizing customer dissatisfaction

Jersey → team's jerseys → Internal competition

When the sales teams are motivated to win an award and recognition, they go the extra mile to win new customers and delight their existing customers. Can there be internal competition between the sales teams of different areas/regions/zones?

11. **Frame**—Salesforce related

From the limited frames in the beginning, largely based on "more" and "better", we have created 11 frames. We have come a long way, isn't it?

Step 4

Adding more dots in the existing frames

For the time being, as an example, we will select one frame – "Processes and system". So far in this frame, we already have two dots – "Mapping customer journey", "Back to basics". To this frame, let's try to add more dots:

1. A mechanism to capture the structured and periodic feedback from the customer.
2. A mechanism to work on customer feedback.
3. In the customer journey, a set of processes built around every touchpoint to enhance the customer experience.
4. A transparent system that enables the customer to escalate his complaints or grievances.
5. Creating a platform that facilitates periodic discussion between the top

customers of the organization and the leadership team.
6. Setting up the forums that allow the field force to share their feedback on customer behavior, preference, area of satisfaction and dissatisfaction, and suggestions.
7. The IT-enabled process to analyze the effectiveness of brand communication.

With the addition of these seven dots, the frame of process and systems will now have nine dots. Similarly, you can add more dots to all the remaining eleven frames.

Step 5

Connecting the diverse dots from different frames

This is the place where one finds breakthrough ideas.

In this case, the hypothetical challenge faced by the client is stated broadly. It doesn't carry the details about the industry, product, competition, etc. Using this hypothetical example, it won't be possible to tell whether the solution we will arrive at will be a differentiated solution. But for the sake of understanding the process, let's combine the dots from different frames and arrive at the idea:

"A cross-functional leadership team, which is part of the strategy, marketing, sales, market research, and new product development, will collectively interact with a set of customers to understand their requirements of the products peripheral to the company's main product range. This initiative will help the company develop a new product range and increase its per customer returns. At the same time, the customers will be happy due to the attention, and in the long run, it will fill their need gap."

In this idea, what are the different frames we have combined?

1. Processes and systems
2. Teamwork
3. Customer feedback
4. Customer delight
5. Business per customer

This way, one can arrive at a list of ideas by combining different frames and selecting the best idea from them.

Phew, that was quite exhaustive.

Thankfully, I have completed my part of heavyweight lifting. Now it's your turn to crack **the ultimate challenge** that I had been talking about and emerge as **the idea machine**!

Exercise

<u>Your Ultimate Challenge</u>

In the beginning, you had listed down the challenges that you need to crack in order to achieve your most important goal.

Your ultimate challenge is to create one hundred dots – generate one hundred ideas to crack your challenges.

Do you find the figure of one hundred too intimidating? It need not be. So far, you have learned so many things. Besides, you have to just **focus on finding new frames**. Once you find enough new frames, you just need to fill them with enough dots to reach one hundred ideas (dots).

For example, find ten new frames and think of ten dots in each of the frames. Or find twenty-five frames and add four dots in each of the frames. Or find fifty frames and add two dots in each of the frames.

Here is good news for you. You are not starting from zero. During some of the previous exercises, you have already created a lot of frames. You just need to bring all of them to one place and add the remaining.

By capturing all the key learnings of previous chapters, let me tell you the steps that you need to follow:

1. **Reversing assumptions:** Earlier, you did the exercise of reversing the assumption. In that exercise, after writing down the opposite statement. You asked yourself, "Why might it be true?" and "How can I make these ideas happen"? When you answer these questions, you find new frames. How

many new frames did you find earlier? Please list them down. Now do the same exercise one more time. Try to find a few more new frames. What is your total now?

2. **Changing your questions:** Like above, earlier at the end of the chapter, "Change Your Frame, Change Your Game", you did the exercise of finding new frames by changing your question. How many new frames did you find earlier? Please list them down. Now do the same exercise one more time. Here you can use the technique of "wearing different hats" to your advantage. Try to find a few more new frames. The more the hats of different people you wear, the more frames you can discover. What is your total now?

3. **Random Words Technique:** In this chapter, by using the random word "bicycle", we created 11 frames, and after connecting the diverse dots from different frames, we created 5 more frames. So, with one random word, we could generate 16 frames. By following the same technique, how many random words would you need to create One hundred frames? You can use as many random words as you can to generate the maximum number of frames.

4. **Adding dots to the frames:** As seen in this chapter, it is easy to add dots

(ideas) to reach the magic figure of one hundred once you have enough frames.
5. **Allow your mind to wander:** You have understood how our subconscious mind feeds us with ideas. At any point in time, you feel that the task has become too daunting for you, allow your mind to wander. When it comes back, it will bring a few golden nuggets (more frames) for you.
6. **Flex your ideas muscle:** You have built strong ideas muscle by doing so many exercises after every chapter. It's time to demand more from it.
7. **Sleep on your challenge:** After a night's sleep, your subconscious mind will not let you stop at one hundred ideas. It will keep on bringing you more and more. Always keep your notepad and pen ready.

Finally, after you cross the magic number of one hundred, do me a favor. Write to me, share your experience. Nothing can be more rewarding for me.

Section # 7 - From Comfort Zone To 10x Zone

Chapter 19 — *From Comfort Zone To 10x Zone*

Isn't it a tragedy that people live their whole life thinking of themselves as non-creative, whereas they have a creative genius residing within them?

Can there be a greater tragedy than this?

Yes, there is.

The greater tragedy is when people get wow ideas but never bring them in front of the world due to the fear of rejection.

Who would know it better than me? As I did the same for several years.

My story

During my early representative days, I used to get lots of creative ideas that I applied during my day-to-day fieldwork. In most instances, those ideas worked quite well. As a result, I started considering myself as a creative type of person.

One day, I saw an ad for a brand that was newly introduced in India. One particular line in its body copy caught my attention. I found that by tweaking, it becomes a great caption for one of our brands. I was quite excited about my creativity.

I thought it was such a powerful idea that I should share it with the right person from the head office. So, when I got a chance to meet the concerned marketing head, I excitedly bounced my thoughts on him.

I had expected him to be equally excited. In my mind, I started dreaming rosy scenarios...my idea had become the central theme of the brand campaign...I am basking in glory...I have come on the radar of the top bosses...and finally, a role in marketing that I had always aspired for. My imagination was running wild.

My interaction with the marketing head didn't exactly happen the way I had imagined. He seemed to be completely unimpressed. However, he was a perfect gentleman. He didn't tell me in so many words that it was a lousy idea. He just listened to me. His face wore a patient expression of a father listening to the rant of his four-year-old son. He then brought up some other topic. This was his polite way of conveying that he thought of my idea as a mediocre one.

I was devastated. My self-image as a creative being came crumbling down. I had made a fool of myself in his eyes. At that very moment, somewhere deep down, below my conscious level, I promised myself that henceforth I would never expose myself to such ridicule. After that, whenever I got any ideas that had a semblance to creativity, I kept them within myself.

A few years back, after dwelling for so many years in a creative field. I remembered this incident and the idea. I took a fresh look at it. And it struck me like a bolt. My idea was indeed a creative one. It was the marketing head who lacked creativity. I wasted many years of my career wrongly believing that I was not a creative type, coupled with my fear of rejection.

What really helped me were some of the techniques I have mentioned in the exercise section. The only regret that I have is that I did not apply them early enough.

Creative ideas need to be acted upon. Because not acting on your ideas is as good as not having any ideas. This may seem like a no-brainer, but in reality, not many people display the courage to present their creative ideas to the world. People are too scared to take their first step into an unknown terrain due to the fear of rejection, both real and imaginary. As a result, millions of ideas that would have made this world a much better place and created a fortune for those who conceived them were never acted upon.

In the introduction, I had quoted Les Brown. I would like to repeat the same once again – *"The wealthiest place on the planet is the graveyard because in the graveyard we will find inventions that we were never ever exposed to, ideas, dreams that never became a reality, hopes and aspirations that were never acted upon."*

Your journey to creativity is never complete unless you overcome this fear of rejection or fear of ridicule.

As we discussed in the beginning, creativity is the long lever that can fetch you 10x results. But creative ideas also need a courageous mind willing to leap from the comfort zone to the 10x zone.

Become rejection proof and leap into the 10x zone

Jia Jing started his journey as an entrepreneur, something that he had dreamt of all his life. He assembled a team of whip-smart engineers. In three months, the team built an app and started using it themselves. By using the app, they were surprised to see the way it boosted their productivity. The team knew that they had a good concept in hand. Jing was looking for investors. He had put most of his savings in his new venture. The time was running out. He had only two months left.

Finally, their product caught investor's attention. The team made a fabulous pitch presentation. At least that's what they thought.

This pitch presentation followed the most agonizing wait that Jia had ever experienced.

Finally, Jia received the mail from the investor. He said no.

He still had two more months. But he realized that this experience had left him terrified of the next debacle.

Jia needed to find some other investor in the next two months. But he realized that he also needed to find something more. A permanent solution to his deep-rooted fear of rejection.

Jia stumbled upon a website called Rejection Therapy. Inspired by it, Jia decided to undertake a hundred days of grueling experience by committing himself to "100 Days of Rejection".

I don't think that I can do justice to Jia's fascinating journey by continuing to write any further. I strongly urge you to watch his Ted talk[1]— What I learned from 100 days of rejection. It will change the way you look at rejections. But don't stop there, buy a copy of his book[2], *Rejection Proof*.

On this high note, I would like to end my book. But not before you start practicing the last final exercise given at the end.

I wish you all the success in your journey towards mastering creativity. If you find any suggestion written in this book useful that impacts you in some way, please write to me. **I will be delighted to read your mail.**

Exercise

Did you watch Jia Jiang's video? I hope you thoroughly enjoyed it.

Won't you like to take the "100 Days of Rejection" challenge?

If you are all game for it and eager to start it immediately. You need not read any further. But if you think his methods are too extreme for your comfort, here is a gentler way. Perhaps you may be ready after this three-week exercise for moving out of your comfort zone.

How will this exercise help you?

Our thoughts and actions create neural pathways inside our brains. When the same set of thoughts and actions are repeated, the neural pathways become deeply ingrained like grooves on a vinyl record. These grooves confine us to a single frame. A simple way of breaking out of it is by consciously doing different actions. These exercises are planned to move you out of your comfort zone without feeling threatened. We will begin slowly, get comfortable with the new experience and after the week, move into the next gear.

Week # 1: Do different things.

In the first week, Just try something different every day. The idea is to bring about the change in an effortless and non-intimidating manner. I am listing a few examples below, just to give you an idea. Once you understand the type of actions that I am referring to, you can add more things to the list.

- In case you are a brand loyalist, try switching to different brands.
- Read a book of a different genre.
- Take a different route to your work.
- Spend your weekend doing a completely new set of activities.
- Go to a different restaurant.
- Order a different type of dish.

Week # 2: Make yourself uncomfortable.

It's time to change gears. In this week, you will practice those activities that would make you somewhat uncomfortable. At the end of the first week, change will already be happening inside you. It will ensure that you will be able to successfully handle a set of uncomfortable activities like the ones below in the second week.

- Try a new hairstyle.
- Change your outfit to wear something you had never imagined.
- Smile at a stranger.
- Start a conversation with a total stranger.
- Upwardly revise your goals.
- Share your feelings, vulnerabilities with others.
- State your expectations or interest to others without sounding apologetic.

Week # 3: Do things that scare you.

There is powerful advice to help you move out of your comfort zone — "Do one thing every day that scares you". It's no doubt a transformative piece of advice. But at times, it can be a paralyzing experience. But you need not worry. The earlier two weeks of activities have already brought about considerable changes within you. Now, you are ready to experience a big change in yourself.

Here is a list of a few of the activities that you should attempt every day. (If you are comfortable with any of the activities listed below, please replace them with a set of activities that scare you a lot.)

- Volunteer to speak in public.
- Dance in public.
- Reach out to well-known figures in case you come across any of them.
- Publicly share your aspirations.
- In seminars, workshops, meetings, or any other public forum, ask lots of questions to get all your doubts clarified, even at the cost of being considered a fool.
- Ask a total stranger for a favor in a calm, matter-of-fact way.
- If you are still not a YouTuber, start your channel. Post your video on it.
- Post something bizarre, unconventional, something that you normally would never do.

Once again, the exercises that I have given in all the above sections are just a few examples for you to get a flavor of expectations for every week. Based on it, you can invent your own challenges that are more appropriate for you. For the third week, you may refer to Jia Jiang's book, Rejection Proof.

References

1. https://www.youtube.com/watch?v=-vZXgApsPCQ
2. https://www.amazon.com/Rejection-Proof-Became-Invincible-Through/dp/080414138X/ref=tmm_hrd_swatch_0?_encoding=UTF8&qid=&sr=

Answers

Chapter 4

The stick puzzle

$$XI + I = X$$

There are three ways you can correct the equation without touching even a single stick:

1. Look at the problem upside down by flipping the book
2. Read it from right to left – X (ten) + I (one) + IX (nine) (You have read the entire book, including the chapter on assumptions. I, therefore, believe that reading it from left to right is no more a big issue for you.)
3. Read the equation by seeing the equation in the mirror.

Half of thirteen

Here are more ways by which thirteen can be divided into two halves.

$$13 \quad \Rightarrow \quad 1 \text{ and } 3$$

XIII = XI and II ⇒ 11 and 2

Thirteen = Thir and teen ⇒ 4 and 4

XIII = ~~XI~~II ⇒ VIII = 8 (upper part of the half)

Chapter 9

The cab driver

Though he was a professional cab driver, he was walking on the road when the incident happened.

The man jumping out of his window

The man lives in a flat that is at ground level.

May I ask you for a small favor?

Could you please leave a review of the book?

One last time!

To put it straight– **reviews are the lifeblood for any author.**

It will just take less than a minute for your, but will tremendously help me to reach out to more people, so please leave your review.

Printed in Great Britain
by Amazon